The Historical Companion to House-Brewing

by

Clive La Pensée

Illustrated by John and Wendy Munday

MONTAG PUBLICATIONS

Published by Montag Publications,
6, Minster Avenue, Beverley, HU17 0NL

Printed by V. Richardson & Sons Ltd.,
Brekkes Buildings, William Wright Dock, Hull, HU3 4PA

ISBN 0 9515685 0 7

CONTENTS

going to the maltsters, who enjoyed a monopoly. Cobbet argued that apart from relieving the hard pressed worker, abolition of the tax would have freed the working man, "from the temptations of the ale house."

The much praised *Deutsche Reinheitsgebot,* was passed in 1516 to protect the innocent drinker from the trickery of unscrupulous brewers who were prepared to add just about anything to a brew to make it go further, increase the drinker's thirst, or improve its narcotic potency. In itself, this law, preventing the use of any ingredients but malt, yeast and hops, was probably most necessary, and similar laws were later passed in England, but they did limit the activities of honest brewers who happened to use a variety of ingredients. These laws generally allowed house-brewing, but often in fact suppressed it.

An example of their effect can be seen by taking Germany again as an example. The dissemination of information on brewing is still forbidden although there is no law against anyone turning his or her kitchen into a brew-house. Hence there are no longer any home-brew books on the market. Commercial breweries however, don't seem to be hampered by this law and books on modern brewing technology abound. This legalised suppression is certainly no new feature in the history of house-brewing and often had its roots in the desire of the landowners and later the rich town gentry to make big commercial killings by monopolising such a basic commodity as beer. The profits from such a rich source flowed into the pockets of the powerful and commercially astute who went to great lengths, fighting fierce competition, in order to secure brewing rights.

As the suppression of home-brewing was also accompanied by the increasing use of hops instead of the traditional Grout, the types of spiced beer available decreased whilst the opportunities for the professional to rip off his customers grew. One knows from many sources that the English drinker did not take to the use of hops immediately and it was oft berated as a "pernicious weed". Hops were in many cases thrust on the drinker but if he wasn't able to resist the demise of his traditional ale, it seems that he did resist his demise as a house-brewer until the 19th century and the rapid industrialisation associated with that time. There are certainly enough sources which indicate that house-brewing was alive and well as late as 1790. The successful suppression seems to have occurred across Europe from that time onwards, usually with the excuse that the house product was inferior to that which the professional master brewer made. This was certainly sometimes the case, but one should set against this the reasons which were often produced by a variety of writers encouraging people, especially the poorer labouring classes, to continue to make their own beer, for by the industrial revolution, beer had become the poor man's drink. He still needed the food and liquid intake commensurate with hard physical labour while his rich employer could afford wine, coffee, and tea. Thus the suppression of house-brewing, coupled with a relative lack of interest in the quality of beer by the ruling industrialist, left the way free for every sort of cheating, and profiteering, including the addition of poisons and narcotics in order to produce "drunkenness", without having to make relatively expensive alcohol. One such writer on this subject was Johann Gottfried Hahn who in his 1804 book published in Erfurt, "House-Brewing, complete with a description of a Brewing Machine,"

complains in the introduction, "Who would not have to agree with me that it is otherwise much stronger and more nutritionally prepared than by us?" His opinion was reinforced by English writers such as Childs in his book, "Everyman his own Brewer". Apart from the sale of too thin beer, Hahn accuses the police of complicity, acceptance of bribes, and nepotism. He had many more complaints and continued, "If we had righteous and disinterested men who never misused their position, who always tried their hardest to make sure that everyone received a healthy, nutritional and fine tasting beverage, one would have no reason to complain and would readily accept and obey the necessary laws. But how seldom is this the case? How often are privileges abused and mostly by the owners and tenants. Is it not avarice in those holding the rights to brew beer, who for full price deliver the county a dishonest and unhealthy imitation, a beverage containing things with such narcotic potency that even the moderate drinker lies drunk and incapable, unable to work, provoked to argue and fight?"

Some English sources of that time indicate that similar circumstances were to be found in this country. Other writers pointed out that with wages, especially those of women, as low as they were in the late 18th century, women were far better employed staying at home and making healthy vitals for the family. Childs even calculated that the family would be in pocket if women rejected the sweat shops and brewed and baked at home.

It had been considered women's work to brew beer since the craft was discovered. In the late Middle Ages the monasteries would frequently employ a woman to do the brewing and in the 18th century the teacher, pharmacist and philosopher Lorenz Crell wrote, "Every rural brewer, every publican in a village pub, every tenant farmer's labourer wants to understand the art. Educated men gape at the insuperable difficulties the common brewer faces while old women are able to make good beer with such ease, for even the number of brewers who commend themselves is most limited".

There is evidence that the professional brewers in England were also women. Mother Louse and Elynoure Rummynge are famous examples of 15th and 16th century "Ale Wives". The latter was so important that she was immortalised in unflattering doggerel by Skelton, a tutor to Henry VIII. Despite his elevated position he still frequented the "Running Horse", in Leatherhead and purchased her ale there along with "travellers, tynkers, sweters and swinkers". On the same subject the English herbalist, Gerard, wrote in 1597, "the women of our Northern Counties, especially in Wales and Cheshire, spice their ale with ivy," and many of us know the nursery rhyme:

I had a little hen,
The prettiest ever seen;
She washed the dishes
And kept the house clean.

She went to the mill
To fetch me some flour,
And always got home
In less than the hour.

She baked me my bread,
She brewed me my ale.
She sat by the fire
And told a fine tale.

Now many feminists will not appreciate the way the qualities of the mediaeval little house mother are being praised, but obviously a properly run household was a valued commodity and the writer of the rhyme may have been patronising but knew how appreciative any man should be, to have a housewife who could brew his ale.

So why another beer book?

I hope that this brief history of the suppression of beer brewing will illustrate some of the things which dependency on commercial brewers has taken from us. The variety of beers and the spices used to flavour them are perhaps our most obvious losses and the home-brew cans have done little to correct this, but also a tradition and a basic foodstuff has been taken from our larders. Although we may not all rush out and brew ivy beer, the recipes and ingredients recommended in the following chapters, and the different malts described, which were once part of various kitchens across Europe, do deserve to be preserved out of historical interest. I hope you will want to try the recipes too!

And the more practical reasons for writing this book. It gives vegans and health food apostles the opportunity to make their own malt and dry their own hops, for so as long as you can secure a reliable source of barley, you can make beer to your own purity standards. But even if you never brew a drop of your own stuff, a thorough understanding of how others do it, will give a more intimate relationship with, and a more critical eye to the beer you buy. But be careful! Once you start on this path there is no going back, and you will end up viewing everything from a washing machine repair or the meal you always took for granted, quite differently. Brewing good beer is followed by making good wine, bread, cheese, keeping goats... It becomes a way of life.

This Companion is meant for the enthusiastic home-brewer and so relatively little space has been given to the basic arts of mashing and sparging. Apart from the fact that there are any number of comprehensive works on basic home-brew techniques on the market, I find one must develop one's own methods to suit the kitchen or outhouse available. Hence only sufficient information is contained to enable one to understand principles and then use personal initiative to solve the technical problems.

Not everything past is good and everything modern to be scorned! Some recipes and methods are included out of historical interest and should be viewed with a critical eye. Some suggestions are downright eccentric and I certainly haven't bothered to brew according to them. Others sound such good fun that every enthusiastic home-brewer will want to give them a try.

Many recipes require malt types which are no longer commercially available. Detailed chapters on historical malting methods, scaled down and adapted for modern kitchens are included as well as extensive information on herb beers and hop surrogates. There are hints on growing and drying a variety of beer spices including details on setting up a hop garden and drying the cones.

The text is richly illustrated with historical diagrams and pictures, many of which have been specially drawn for this publication by John and Wendy Munday.

I have always been assisted in historical research by my wife Eva, without whose tireless searches through the decentralised West German library system, many of the Continental recipes would never have come to light. I am also indebted to my late colleague Oberstudienrat Fritz Sommer, whose translations of recipes from Medieval Low German have enabled this Companion to contain detailed brews spanning 500 years.

It was never conceivable that I should be able to try such an incredible variety of recipes and techniques but I have worked up all the available information and present it in a form which allows one to tackle any one of them in a modern kitchen. This was often done with a heavy heart as I feel that I cannot do justice to openings such as, "Soak six quarters of best barley..." or "Wede wyl oltbeer wol waren dat dar het sponbeer de schal nemen unde hoeulen spone und bynden in bundekin..."

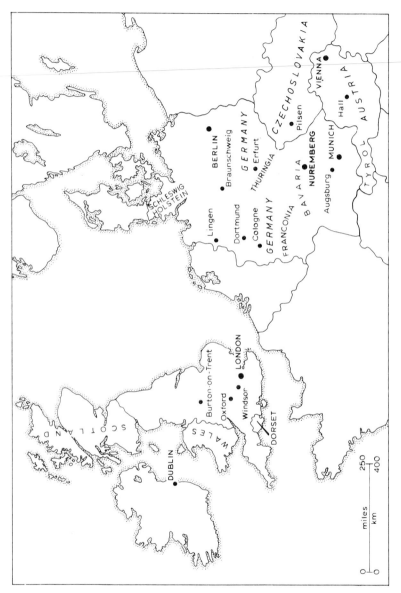

Some of the famous towns and regions for malting and brewing

2. Types of Beer.

Beers of the British Isles.

The UK and Irish Republic are probably the only countries to still brew all their traditional beers using top fermenting yeasts. Without going into detail here on the meaning of this term, it does supply a ready made division between us and the rest. These beers also happen to be the easiest to brew and so are of especial interest to the home-brewer. They use a relatively simple infusion method, and the top fermenting yeasts require temperatures which are readily available in most kitchens. So try a few British brews before venturing to the continental recipes at the back of the book.

The easiest of the English beers to make is probably Ale. This is the oldest beer, also known to the old Germanics and finds mention in the Eddalied as the drink of the common folk, called Aloin in Old Nordic. The Gods however drank beer, from the Norse Bior. Hops arrived in Britain with the Dutch immigrants of the early 16th century. There are much quoted rhymes about their arrival. One version is

> Hops, Reformation, bays and beer
> Came to England all in one year.

whereas another claims

> Tyrkeys, Carps, Hops, Piccarel and Beer,
> Came to England in one year.

Whatever these versatile Lowlanders all brought in one or probably more years, beer was not an immediate success. Ale remained the name for the traditional unhopped drink spiced with varieties of herbs or mixtures of herbs called the Grout. The word "beer", described the new-fangled foreign concoction which was spiced with hops. It seems that the traditional drinker rigorously defended his ale and even if it held second place in Europe, it remained throughout Tudor times the principle brew in England. Eventually the grout gave way to hops but ale has remained in our vocabulary and is as popular as ever although spiced with hops since several hundred years.

Ale is now brewed in many different strengths. Light Ale is a pale, strongly hopped beer of about 3.7% alcohol content with an unfermented wort relative density of about 1.030. Pale Ale has a higher wort density and Mild Ale a lower one. The latter, and Brown Ale, have a stronger colour because of the addition of darker malts. Old Ale as the name implies, is stored longer, thus allowing enzyme activity to have a greater effect on the nature of the beer.

Bitter is the most popular of the British beers and it is made with pale malts and relatively large amounts of hops. Untutored foreigners pull faces as if they are about to be poisoned by this strange tasting and flat beverage, but usually the necessary practice proves our point. This is the beer which was supposed to have been responsible for the peculiar opening times which British pubs have kept. Due to the large amount of hops used in bitter it makes drinkers rather sleepy and so that the war effort wasn't hindered the pubs around Woolwich were shut in the afternoons. A nice story which I haven't been able to substantiate but certainly the Defence of the Realm Act 1914 made it an offence to make servicemen on duty drunk and the Temporary Restriction Act 1914 gave licensing justices the power to vary and curtail opening hours.

Barley Wine is probably the strongest beer brewed in the United Kingdom and with a 10% alcohol content, is better left in the bottle or drank like a wine. Stout is another beer which bemuses foreigners. It is still most popular in Ireland which is also the home of the most famous stout of all, Guinness with its nearly black colour and head with the consistency of whipped cream. If you manage to brew a stout in whose head you can write your name with a cocktail stick you have definitely arrived as a brewer! Stouts get their bitter, slightly wooden taste from the large quantity of burnt malt which is used. They also have a very high nutritional value and so called Milk Stouts are a meal in themselves with added non-fermentable lactose sugar. These are traditionally served to feeding mothers, and as some stouts contain 5% alcohol they are reputed to quieten the feeding baby, although if this were true the amounts the mother had drunk would be extremely bad for her and the baby.

Porter is an elusive drink which everyone knows about but nobody drinks. In the course of this book you will find many definitions of Porter and they may all be correct, or have been correct at some time or another. The Oxford Dictionary says it is a dark brown bitter brewed from charred or browned malt that perhaps was originally brewed for stevedores and market workers. H. A. Monckton in his scholarly book on the history of English ale and beer tells that at the end of the 16th century, three hopped ales were common; a dark ale which was highly hopped and not a particular commercial success, pale ale which was brewed with best quality pale malt and correspondingly expensive and so failed as an intended competitor to the dark ale, and old ale. The brown ale brewers tried to improve their market share with a more heavily hopped competitor product of their own, but it took a long time to mature and tied up too much capital. Furthermore the fickle drinking public preferred a 50:50 mixture of any two of the three. In 1720 the brewers decided to produce one beer with the qualities of the sought after mixture. This was an immediate success, especially with the London porters, hence the name. Thus in its original form as a mixture of different beers it was not known as porter and may not always have been spiced with hops. For the last 260 years it has been brewed from its own recipe, except that I know of no brewery in the U.K. brewing it.

Porter has always been popular in Ireland and is mentioned frequently in folk music and literature of that country. It is one of the few English beer recipes to have been exported and at the beginning of the 19th century was copied in Germany. North German brewers made it so strong that few porters could have done a days work after imbibing. A recipe of a fearfully strong porter, or at least

16

what 18th century German brewers thought was porter, is included in the recipes in chapter 9.

Talking of mixing beers, this is still common practice in the UK. Londoners can be heard ordering "Mild and Bitter", and in Liverpool and the East Riding "Brown Mixed", has retained its popularity, being a mixture of brown ale and bitter. "Black and Tan", has become something of a rarity.

Continental Beers

There can be no doubt that German Beers have gained the most popularity, at first on the continent and now world-wide, and certainly enjoy the best reputation for quality. One should not infer that other countries don't brew excellent beers. After all, popularity is only of interest to the large breweries.

The most important European beers are the bottom fermenters which are generally known as Lager Beers. This name reminds us that these beers need relatively long times to mature. (Germ. lagern, to store). They are fermented with a yeast strain called Saccharomyces Carlsbergensis which has the ability to remain active at temperatures close to zero centigrade. At these very low temperatures the solubility of the fermentation product, carbon dioxide, is much higher than at room temperature and gives rise to the head (Blume) which we associate with them. This also accounts for the hostile looks Germans give our flatter beverages but then it takes a foreigner to insist on a mouth full of foam and a belly full of gas before they smile.

The commercially most important German beer which now enjoys world wide popularity is Pils which takes its name from the Czechoslovakian town of Pilsen, where it first became popular. It has become a most important German and Belgian export and was originally made from extremely pale malt which requires the very soft water found in Pilsen, and moderate amounts of Saaz hops. It is typified by the high dissolved carbon dioxide concentration and an alcohol content of 4.5-5%. Pils is often confused with Dortmunder Bier which is made from slightly darker malt, less hops and contains over 5% alcohol. These two beers are highly popular in Middle and North Germany but mention must also be made of the Bavarian types which, because of the Oktoberfest have become equally famous. Many light beers are now common place in Bavaria but the original Münchener Bier is dark. The reason for this lies in the water which allows the use of strongly roasted malts. Its alcohol content is also around 5%. More important to the fame of Bavarian beers are perhaps the special beers which are brewed for festive occasions. Since the Middle Ages beers such as Bockbier, with an alcohol content of up to 12%, have been brewed for Lent. They also contain a lot of soluble malt extract, including starch, and so are a form of "liquid bread", for liquids don't break the fast.

Another speciality are the Rauchbiere which actually taste of the burnt beechwood chippings over which the malt is dried and roasted. These beers need a maturing time of at least three years and so much patience will be needed if you want to try to make one.

There are also some top fermenting types made in Germany. In Westphalia a dark Altbier is served in small glasses and if you ask for Bowle it will be served with either strawberries, or pineapple pieces floating in it and it tastes very good too! In Cologne a very light top fermenter is made called Kölsch and how drinkers of that dare turn their noses up at bitter is beyond me.

Beers made from wheat have not been produced in the UK for many years but some commercially brewed wheat beers are still available in Germany. Berliner Weißbier and the South German Weizenbier represent this unusual species. They are all fermented with the yeast strain Saccharomyces Cerevisiae which is only really active above about 16°C. Apart from the weaker Berliner Weiße, all these types contain around 5% alcohol. As wheat beers tend to have a slightly sour taste, people outside Berlin have been known to add strawberries and the like to their Weißbier but true Berliners would never stoop to such depths. They would perhaps hang in a little woodruff in May and then drink it from a strange contraption rather resembling a reject Champagne glass.

With imagination and flexibility, the recipes given in this book should allow the brewing of similar beers to those mentioned in this chapter. Of greater interest however must be the beers which one can no longer buy. Oat Ale, Porter, Farrenbacher Weißbier, Schleswig Holstein Gruel Beer from the 17th century, of such simplicity that 15 minutes in the kitchen, followed by two days fermentation renders it ready to drink, Twopenny Ale, or a Mum Ale, possibly dating from the 15th century; these must be our most sought after prizes and you will need no special equipment that cannot be fabricated from a plastic bucket and a brass tap, except maybe some stone or earthenware tankards. Before the invention of glass nobody cared if the beer was cloudy so why should we?

3 The Road to Factory Brewing

"Ill customs have greater power over Mankind, than either the Law of God or Nature, but Wisdom is justified of her children."

(Thomas Tryon, 1691. Student in Physick and celebrated brewer.)

A definition of what beer is would be useful at this point but unfortunately any such attempt is going to be an over-simplification. In 1939 the German "Biersteuergesetz," laid down by law that a bottom fermenting beer may only be made from barley malt, hops and water, using alcoholic fermentation. In the early 15th century, tradition in England was reinforced by law and ale was defined as consisting of only malt, usually from barley, water and yeast and presumably some form of flavouring. Hops were a much later addition but not until 1847 did an Act of Parliament allow the use of additional sugar. This legal huffing and puffing begged the fact that brewers across Europe frequently used grits (other starch sources), and around the world beer has been made since the beginning of sedentary societies from every imaginable type of starch and every conceivable and inconceivable form of flavouring including poisons and narcotics. Thus in Africa millet beer is common, East Asia, rice, and in South America maize is used. Historians also believe that all these societies discovered brewing independently of each other and Europe.

Although we will not restrict ourselves in our brewing efforts to the most recent German definition, as most European beers adhere approximately to it, I shall assume its validity for the moment.

Malting

All seeds store the energy they will need to start growing in the form of starch. When the seed is planted and there is sufficient warmth and moisture available for germination to commence, specific enzymes present in the seed for the purpose, begin to change the starch to a more readily usable form of energy, sugar. The barley seed makes the sugar called maltose and this is what the brewer will finally ferment. The enzymes only become active when the seed begins to germinate. If the water content of the seed is below 5% then it will remain indefinitely dormant. The purpose of malting is to germinate the seed under controlled conditions to produce and activate the required enzymes. Once the enzymes are present, the maltster dries the germinating barley thus rendering them inactive again. The maltster only wants to get the barley enzymes in a usable state. It is the brewer's task to actually convert any starch to sugar. The germinating barley is called green malt and the dried, enzyme inactive product is known as malt. Thus the maltster is merely speeding up a process which occurs in nature. Theoretically any type of cereal can be used to make malt but in practice barley is best.

The barley is first steeped in a cistern containing cold water until it has increased its water content from about 3% (dormant state) to about 45% (ready to grow). This takes around three days. As the barley becomes active it respires and produces carbon dioxide gas. To prevent it "suffocating", on this waste product, air is blown through the cistern, or the water frequently changed.

The swollen barley is drained of water and either loaded onto trays or floors, or more usually nowadays into drums which rotate. Whatever method is chosen the barley must be frequently moved to allow the passage of fresh air around the seeds. This turning the floor used to be a full time job requiring much skill to judge the progress of the enzyme production. Rounded wooden instruments and bare feet were the order of the day for turning as these cause least damage to the barley. Once the first roots appear as tiny white "eyes" (called chitting), one knows germination has successfully been commenced. Germination begins very quickly and is allowed to continue until the young roots and the acrospire (first leaf) have reached a certain length. Turning the floor now becomes difficult because the roots will form a thick interwoven mat if allowed to, and then the green malt may suffocate or spoil as the heap becomes too hot. Experience has shown the point at which the most enzymes have been produced and to prevent the seed consuming more starch, the germination is stopped by drying. The water content of the so called green malt is slowly reduced to about 5-10% because the enzymes cannot tolerate high temperatures whilst still wet. The heap still needs to be turned during this gentle kilning phase and this must have been a most unpleasant task as the traditional firing materials were wood, straw and later coke. The man doing the turning would be subjected to the fumes and smoke for many hours a day. Further drying to about 1.5% water content at higher temperatures terminates all remaining life in the malt and renders it suitable for storing. This final "roasting" destroys some of the protein and carbohydrates in the corn and leaves the malt with its typical smell and taste. Variations in drying and roasting temperatures produce the variety of malts required for diverse types of beer. The malt is finally cleaned to remove the roots.

Malting large batches of barley cannot have been a pleasant task. It was very hard work, and a few moments dilatoriness or rough handling of the barley could cause overheating, mould or waste of valuable corn substance. No wonder then that the 20th century has seen a massive rationalisation of this process, especially as the demand for malt has increased so radically. Barley may now be steeped in water containing chemicals which allow the biochemistry to continue but restrict the growth of the roots and acrospire, thus reducing the amount of corn substance used to commence germination. The tedious drying process has received much attention from chemical engineers but in the seventies there was a considerable scare on the Continent about the high nitrosamine content of the beer due to these modern techniques. Typical claims and counter claims ensued about risks of cancer etc. The poor consumer can only guess who got it right. The beauty of the old maltsters method is that it can be carried out in any shed, barn or kitchen, allows the maltster to make his own special house brand and provided one doesn't try to cope with too larger batches at once, is not particularly hard work. Making malt is a great deal of fun though.

Skidby Mill, East Yorkshire, Interior -
where one can still take malt for grinding.

Mashing and making the wort.

Malt is delivered to the brewer after it has matured for a few weeks, although it keeps many months if stored in a dry place. The malt must first be crushed before the brewer can use it. Malt is very hard and difficult to break. Prior to the use of wind or water power for milling it was ground in a quern at home and must have been an awesome chore. With the widespread use of wind power in the

Middle Ages, the brewers stood in line with bakers and used the communal or manorial windmill and paid a toll. The particle size in the crushed malt is critical. The consequences of allowing the malt grains to be reduced to a fine flour are horrific, for the brewer that is, not the miller and great attention will be given to the various methods which used to be used for dealing with badly ground malt. It is a problem likely to beset the modern house-brewer. Every brewer had his own technique for preparing the malt for milling in order to get the most out of the miller for the least money but all such tricks altered the nature of the final beer. Modern day home-maltsters will not be able to avail themselves of a mill and in the absence of a suitable kitchen machine, he will be back to the quern and may care to develop a few tricks to ease the chore of grinding. In this way he develops his own unique house-brew. Understandably the commercial brewer cannot be doing with relying on tricks or chance and so the malt is ground to very precise specifications but of course the charm and excitement of the unexpected disappears for all but the home-maltster.

Within hours of crushing, the malt was placed in water between 50-75 °C depending on the type of malt available and the beer which was to be made from it. Interestingly, modern treatises on brewing quote 66-71 °C as values for mashing and this again illustrates the narrow outlook of commercial enterprises whose aim has to be optimisation. At these temperatures the starch in the malt is converted most quickly by the enzymes into dextrines (polysaccharides) and then into maltose (a disaccharide). The wider temperature band quoted reflected the need to use varying techniques to cope with poorer quality malts and the lack of accurate temperature measurement, which in themselves lead to an abundance of recipes and beers sorts.

This conversion process of starch into sugar is called mashing and the sugar solution extracted from the malt is referred to as the wort. At the same time as the starch is broken down so are the proteins, pectins and glutens in the grain and as their molecular size decreases they are rendered at least partially soluble in water. These substances provide the beer with its nutritional value. Time is money to the commercial brewery and because the home-brewer can take more time over mashing, his beer contains more goodness. Furthermore the home brewer can determine what grits are used in the mash and how much sugar is added to the wort prior to boiling. A better, more nutritional product is obtained which in turn means you will need to drink less of your house-brew. A pint is a meal and satisfies without the blowout effect of commercial brews.

Flavouring

When the brewer judges all the starch to have been turned to sugar, the wort is drained from the draff (malt residue) and the latter well washed with a fine spray of fresh hot water, a process known as sparging. Washing the draff serves two purposes. It removes the valuable sugar from the malt husks and encourages a sort of after-mash to take place. Until the end of the last century it was common practice to simply remash the draff in order to be sure that as much corn substance as possible is turned into soluble and useful product. Only then did sparging begin. Second or even third mashes have now fallen from favour,

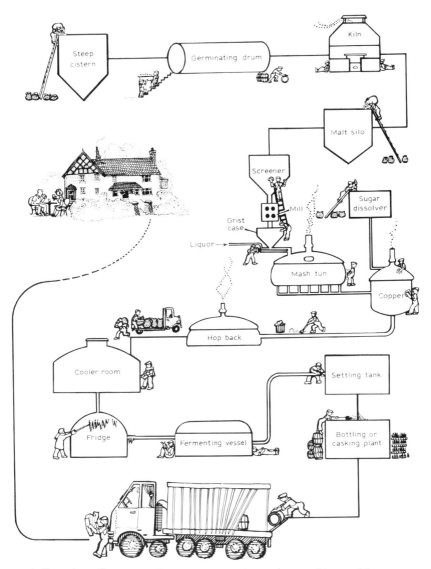

A flow chart illustrating the various steps in modern malting and brewing.

probably because modern mash techniques are so effective that they have rendered multiple mashing unnecessary.

The liquid extract so gained, made up of wort and sparge water, was boiled for anything between 8 minutes and 8 hours with hops, hop surrogates and many other medicinal or non-medicinal herbs, pine shavings, even cherry stones. Sometimes the herbs were simply hung in the wort for a few hours.

If a beer is to keep, then the boiling is essential in order to sterilise the wort but it was not always boiled, perhaps because the people liked it with only a hint of flavour, or the herbs were so pungent that a little was sufficient. Maybe they sometimes simply couldn't afford the firing wood. If it was boiled, which was certainly the most common practice, it needed to be cooled quickly to minimise the risk of infection by air born bacteria or wild yeasts, prior to filtration and fermentation. The longer the wort is cooked and the faster the subsequent cooling, the more of the slow or non-fermentable proteins, glutens and carbohydrates coagulate and precipitate out. This leads to a thinner beer, but one which clears much quicker and more comprehensively: good news for the "time is money" conscious brewer and his public who have been educated to believe that cloudy beer is poisonous. However before the days of refrigeration and when firewood was at a premium, necessity provided for a beverage which was probably a meal in itself, full of such suspended solids.

Nowadays only hops are used for flavouring and the boiling rarely exceeds one hour. Hops have several definite advantages. They preserve the beer, improve its clarity and help the head retention.

The sweet, spiced wort is cooled very quickly and fermented. This young beer is bottled or casked and kept until mature which means anything between 6 weeks and a few years, depending on the type and strength of the beer. It used to be common to serve beer only a few days old and this certainly tasted quite different to what we now expect at our local. What do we expect to find in the can of malt extract on the home brew shelf of our local supermarket? Instead of cooling the spiced wort the cooking is continued until a concentrate results. This is canned and sold as a thick treacly substance. Apart from it being a dreadful waste of energy to boil water off so that the customer may take it home and dilute it with water, I don't believe that this treatment does the hops any good at all or that we profit from purchasing a standardised product.

The complete process of malting and brewing is illustrated on a flow chart of the above mentioned processes as carried out in mechanised breweries. The ancient Egyptians also recorded their endeavours using flow charts. A detail is shown of a wall painting found in the tomb of Kenamon in Schech abdel-Gurna. The bottom row of pictures illustrate huge flat bread-cakes being broken into pieces and placed in a large mash-tub in which the bread is well stamped into the water. Barley, oats, wheat or millet may have been used as starch sources. To the right, great pots are being cleaned and smeared with grease or wax to reduce their porosity. In the second picture row, the mash is being carried to a man at a large sieve who is supervising the kneading and washing of the draff. The top strip shows the filling of the beer into stone storage or drinking vessels. Flavourings used at the time may have been dates, honey, juniper, mushrooms or tree bark depending upon availability. Up till now I have only failed to find a recipe for a mushroom beer. The closest I have come is a bread dough made with beer instead of water and spiced with the rare mushroom *Pleurotus ostreatus* in a German book on cooking with mushrooms. Such beers would have been drunk very new at a festivity or sold from an open air pub. The Egyptians were very knowledgeable in the art of creating a healthy environment and the spices and herbs used in beer may have reflected their desire to create an ambience conducive to spiritual and bodily well-being. They were great recorders and hence we know they used opium and henbane as sedatives and maybe beer as a vehicle for taking such drugs.

The bread cakes used by the Egyptians contained no enzymes to break the starch down as these would have been destroyed by the baking process. Presumably some other malted or unmalted grain was added to the mash to supply the enzymes. The bread may have been chewed well before it went into the mash-tub, for our saliva contains the same enzymes, for the same purpose, to break down starch into sugar. This method of getting the extra enzymes needed into the mash is still used by some African brewers because their starch source, millet, does not contain sufficient natural enzyme.

Try chewing a little white bread for 5 minutes and you will taste it becoming sweet. If you then spit the chewed bread into your mash tub as the ancient Egyptians may have done, and some African tribes still do, I guarantee your friends and neighbours will refrain from drinking all your house-brew for you!

The ancient Egyptians recorded their endeavours on flowcharts too.

Alecost.

Tanacetum Balsamita.

4. The Ingredients.

Malting Barley.

"The grain was steeped and germinated, by which its spirits were excited and set free; it was then dried and ground and infused with water, when after fermentation, it produced a pleasant, warming, strengthening and intoxicating liquor."

The above description, translated from the Geoponius, purports to describe how the ancient Britons used their barley. They probably also used other corns than barley but it was the need to secure a regular supply of cereals for bread and beer making that caused man to cease wandering in search of food and form sedentary communities. According to Juluis Ceasar's description of the early Britons, developed agriculture was only to be found in some coastal areas of the country but there is a quern in the British Museum which predates the Roman invasion, so the grinding of cereal for gruels and bread and beer making, must have been well established by then. I. A. Richmond describes in his book on Roman Britain that Cunobelinus, the founder of Colchester in A.D. 10, had coins struck with himself on one side and a grain of corn on the other, "reminding us not only that this was the natural product of the Essex acres but that the contemporary geographer Strabo mentioned corn as one of the principle British exports," along with, "cattle, gold, silver and iron, hides, slaves and clever hunting dogs." Perhaps the Roman invaders only saw what they wanted to for it would seem that developed communities were well established exporters of surpluses before Ceasar's reports.

Beer was actually a competitor to wine which, although simpler to produce was much more expensive. Nothing is known of the properties or qualities of these early beers, but the use of grain for making beer is again recorded in the fourth century. Richmond also points out that Pytheas had noted in the 4th century B.C. that corn was harvested whilst still green in Britain, threshed and then parched that it keep. "The plan of these kilns and their flues varied considerably, now bowl shaped, now T-shaped, now H-shaped and now forked. But the principle of construction was always the same, to create a fire whose hot gases passed through flues and heated gently a floor, never itself in direct contact with the flame." It is quite apparent then that the Ancient Britons possessed the technology to make malt long before the Roman invasion. In fact the above description means they certainly, at least inadvertently, made malt, for if they gathered their corn wet and left it lying around or took too long over the drying, it will have germinated and the drying process been that of the maltster!

In order to make the variety of beers described in this book, it is necessary to malt your own barley. This is not difficult, but first you must buy the barley. For city dwellers this can appear to be a considerable hurdle but all good home brew shops can obtain malting barley and it is not expensive. The only problem is

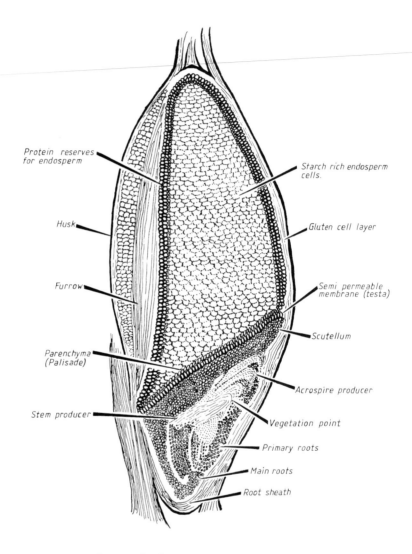

Protein reserves
for endosperm

Starch rich endosperm
cells.

Husk

Gluten cell layer

Furrow

Semi permeable
membrane (testa)

Scutellum

Parenchyma
(Palisade)

Acrospire producer

Stem producer

Vegetation point

Primary roots

Main roots

Root sheath

Longitudinal cross-section of a barley corn.

that one has to buy about 25 kg. as a minimum quantity. In case you don't use a home brew source here are a few pointers on what to look for.

Only the best two rowed summer barley is nowadays considered suitable for malting and this usually grows in mild areas with relatively long reliable summers. The eastern counties of England, Franconia and Bavaria in Germany are favourites. Anyone visiting these areas and thinking of malting at home, should buy themselves a half hundredweight (approximately 50 kg.) as it is very cheap and if kept dry and away from mice etc. will keep several months. Searches in the Yellow Pages under "Agricultural Merchants", are worthwhile and if they can't supply you then they'll know who can. If you use a seed or agricultural merchant be sure to tell him what it is for as seed is treated with a fungicide and is unfit for brewing.

Cereals are basically made up of a husk, containing starch and the necessary apparatus to germinate and develop into a new plant. An in depth understanding of the processes involved when the grain begins to grow is not essential. What is important is that the barleycorn has an additional protective layer which covers and protects the emerging white tip of the first leaf, often called the acrospire. Because barley must be turned during malting to allow air into the seed, prevent it becoming too hot or the roots matting, this protection is essential. If one tries malting wheat in order to make some of the special German beers, it soon becomes apparent how difficult it is to turn the wheat corn without damaging the acrospire and consequently killing the corn. Wheat in fact looses this protective layer as chaff during the ripening process. This accounts for the virtual monopoly barley has in beer making.

The essential parts of the corn can be recognised with a hand lens but a microscope will reveal the starch particles as oval, spherical or lentil shaped, with a cross-sectional size of between $0.02 - 0.035$ mm. They make up about 60% of the total corn substance. Starch is a polysaccharide, i.e. several thousand glucose units chemically joined to each other in a chain structure. The various protective coatings on the corn are made up of cellulose which is also a polysaccharide but the sugar units are differently spacially orientated and contain different functional groups to starch. Iodine solution forms an unmistakable deep blue colour with starch whereas other polysaccharides produce either no colour or lighter reds or blues. Barley also contains small amounts of fat (3.5%), proteins, dextrines and sugars and of course, water.

Although the dried barley can be stored for many years without appearing to go off, in fact it loses its ability to germinate fairly quickly and in a three year old barley sample only half as many seeds will germinate as in a fresh one. The latter should contain at least 98% germinable corn.

There is a never ending list of criteria by which one can measure the quality of a barley sample, but nowadays, provided you get what is asked for, malting barley for brewing, you should be satisfied with your purchase. Be sure to buy this year's harvest in autumn.

Other starch sources.

Only purists who want to brew German bottom fermenters will refuse to use other sources of starch than barley. Many brewers outside Germany supplement their barley with whatever starch is on the market and this is often controlled by the harvest. Economics doubtless changed the law in 1847 to allow grits and sugar to be used legally in the U.K. but this was probably only a recognition of a de facto: malt surrogates were in widespread use anyway. The much hated malt tax was an added incentive to use alternatives to malted barley and there had long been a move to using raw grains. In 1891 the cost of extracting sugar from barley malt was estimated at 5.45d/lb., 3.68d/lb. from unmalted barley, and 2.53d/lb. from maize. Rice, maize and oats are frequently used as grits and the recipes in the back of this book contain a method for brewing a pure oat beer which was brewed in the eighteenth century after a poor barley harvest. Careful scrutiny of the label on home-brew extracts reveals that they too are often a mixture of malt and barley extract and one's pallet may be surprised when a genuine pure barley malt home-brew is served for we are no longer accustomed to its taste. The famous writer on German brewing techniques, Luers, recorded with some amazement how good some of the beers were during the war years, when any surplus or available starch was used for brewing, but despite their general acceptance, they are but a weak imitation of a pure malt beer. This explains why the products Luers referred to would not have been called "Bier", as this title is governed by German law as only being a drink from barley malt, yeast, water and hops and those who brew by German definition a "Bier", understandably try to jealously guard against their product being lumped together with anything containing grits.

Although rice and maize contain 80-85% starch, sago 75-90%, potatoes 65-75% and oats and rye between 60-70%, the problem is how to convert them to fermentable sugar. These starches are either too heavy to be broken down sufficiently for brewing purposes or the seeds naturally contain insufficient enzyme for successful starch/sugar conversion for malting and brewing. This problem was frequently solved by boiling the starch in order to dissolve it or at least suspend it in water. This suspension was mixed with malt which of course contains the important enzyme diastase which can then break down the starch into fermentable sugar. Luers records the preparation of a particularly enzyme rich malt which he called "Kraftmalz", (strong malt) suitable for sorting out and breaking down the very pastiest of potato starches into sugar. Essentially the barley was steeped, then couched until chitting commenced and roots appeared but the acrospire was allowed to continue to grow until it was two or three times the length of the parent seed. Normally growth is stopped before the first leaf exceeds ⅔ the length of the seed, that is before it even appears from under the husk. This Kraftmalz is especially enzyme rich and was mixed with available grits in order to make alcoholic drinks which weren't derived only from barley. Making a special malt isn't really necessary unless one really insists on using potatoes or millet. Ordinary barley malt is adequate if a ½ lb maize or rice is mixed with a ¼lb malt in two litres of water. This is mashed for 30 minutes at 45 °C and then finally boiled gently for 15 minutes. The grit can then be mixed with the main mash out of malt.

When one sees the lengths European brewers go to in order to be able to use cheaper, more readily available starches, one has more respect for the inventiveness of those African women sitting round the mash tub, chewing the millet.

Sugar.

Strictly speaking sugar is not an ingredient in brewing, but an essential intermediate in the process, produced by mashing malt and with the help of yeast is converted into alcohol and carbon dioxide. It became an ingredient during the last century when the increasing use of the saccharometer revealed that dark malts used for colouring actually supplied little else but colour to the beer. This made them a very expensive option and as by 1812 it was realised that the same effect could be achieved with brown sugar or caramel, these were quickly introduced and a new branch of the brewing industry emerged. It was common practice to put all sorts in beer and as the abuses of common sense seem to have been reaching something of an climax by 1816, beer was defined by law as a drink only to be made from malt, hops and yeast. Sugar colourings were felled by the same legal axe. Not until 1847 were sugars sanctioned for use in beer.

Most home-brewers supplement their valuable malt extract by adding a small amount of sucrose (household granulated sugar). It is cheap, ferments easily and provided not too much is added, does not seem to influence the quality of the finished product. 1 kg. sugar to 2.5 kg. unmashed malt seems to be a safe

quantity and should be added during the boiling of the wort. Too much sugar produces a thin nasty little beer, good only for rapid drunkenness and wicked hangovers.

Brown sugar is as good as granulated sugar and gives the beer a little more colour. It doesn't influence the taste.

Glucose is expensive and only used by modern home-brewers who want to spare no cost. Glucose is a mono-saccharide, and the basic building block from which starch is made. Thus purists feel it to be closer to the real thing than sucrose, which is not naturally made in the mash-tun. Neither though is glucose made by mashing. Malt produces the disaccharide maltose and as far as the chemistry of the process is concerned, glucose is as good or bad as the much cheaper sucrose. The only genuine advantage which glucose offers is that it does get the yeast cells working quickly but brewing is about love for the product, not speed of production. That can be purchased in the pub.

Lactose is an interesting variant as it is a non-fermentable sugar and so leaves the beer tasting sweet. It is used to make milk stouts or the German Nährbiere, and is appreciated by feeding mothers and convalescents. Lactose is only available through chemists and has become rather expensive for everyday use.

The brewer who likes experimenting may like to try brown treacle which is certainly cheap enough but apart from altering the colour of the beer, does impart its own flavour and may not be to every taste. Treacle doesn't always ferment too well and is best added to the wort when fermentation is well established.

Honey was the only sugar available to pre-seventeenth century brewers and has certainly been used since brewing began. It was always an expensive option and can only be recommended for use in herbal beers.

Malt extract can be bought in many health food shops, is cheap (well it won't cause you to weep into your beer) and is an authentic sugar surrogate.

Water.

"What Water is best to make Mault? Running or River Water is to be preferred before either Spring, Well or Pond Water, which do contain a certain Unctuous Virtue, or Saline Fatness, that it attracts or draws from the surface of the Earth... besides River Waters have not only the benefit of motion, but also the benevolent Influences of the Coelestial Bodies running in the open air and Light of Heaven which do by its fine vapours penetrate and purge it from its harsh Earthly Qualities..."

Tryon in 1690 had no doubt about the water he wanted his barley steeped in but he could have saved himself a couple of sides in his fascinating treatise "The Art of Brewing Ale and other Malt Liquors", by simply stating "there must be plenty of air in it and not too soft!" River water, because of its open surface, movement, and passage between and over rocks, is the most likely source to be saturated with air and contain plenty of dissolved salts. The dissolved salts cause "hardness", in the water and are dissolved up as rain water flows over rock into streams, rivers and lakes. These salts slow down the rate at which corn substance can leach out of the barley during the steep. What Tryon and generations before him had discovered by empirical trial and error, we are now able to put a scientific explanation to.

We are luckier than Tryon because our tap water is usually ideally suited to malting. It may contain too much chlorine, which is added by the Water Board to disinfect the water but if the steeping bucket is aerated during the process, as described in the chapter on malting, this shouldn't be a problem. If you live in an area with very soft water, you may either harden it as described in appendix 1 or simply accept a slightly lower malt yield and quality.

The choice of water for mashing is not nearly so easily dealt with for it is not chance that certain types of beer are connected with certain towns. Most breweries are where they are because there was to be found the right water for that particular beer. Burton-on-Trent for example has long been famous for its Pale Ales and study of the water reveals a fairly high concentration of calcium sulphate. It would be wrong to say that one can only brew a good Pale Ale with Burton type water, but beers of the same type brewed with another quality water will produce a quite different tasting drink. London waters come from a variety of sources, rivers and springs but much of the water is rich in calcium hydrogen carbonate and sodium chloride. Every type of beer is brewed in London these days but before the knowledge delivered by the water chemist enabled breweries to so diversify, London was particularly noted for Porters and Stouts. Calcium sulphate and calcium chloride rich water produce Mild Ales of note.

Not even I would move house to get the right water for the beer I want, so it is important for the home-brewer to know what type of beer can most successfully be brewed from the water at his disposal. However, brewing with the "wrong" water may well produce a satisfactory drink but it will not have the taste associated with that particular beer type.

Water is generally divided into four groups according to the types and quantities of dissolved salts:

a) soft:- containing little or no dissolved salts.

b) permanently hard:- containing salts of calcium and magnesium which are not removed by boiling the water.

c) temporarily hard:- containing appreciable amounts of calcium hydrogen carbonate which can be removed by boiling. This precipitates the hydrogen carbonate ions as calcium carbonate which explains the use of the name "carbonate hardness", to describe this type of hardness.

d) water containing both the salt types described above.

The latter is most commonly found in the UK. If you are going to worry about the type of water in your area and how it will affect the beer you brew, then get a water analysis from the Water Board and decide which beer is suited to your area and brew it! Who wants the easy way though, when for a little effort more we can take the kitchen sink out of action for hours at a time, adjusting our water to make a Bavarian "Braunbier", from 1842 and drive our spouses to distraction? (You will have just had the baking oven for finishing off the malt!)

Soft water.

Soft water contains very little dissolved salts, tastes rather insipid, produces unending lather with soap and doesn't fur your kettle. Very soft water is rare unless you are prepared to plunder the rain butt. This used to be common practice as it was a source of very clean water when other supplies were less reliable than nowadays. Should you live in a soft water area then light, strongly hopped beers are the natural choice. Careful addition of small quantities of soluble salts of calcium and magnesium in the form of the chloride or sulphate will allow you to achieve permanent hardness and a Dortmund or Burton beer would be possible.

Temporary hardness cannot be created without a supply of carbon dioxide gas. This is then beyond the scope of most home brewers but if you really have to have a go then stir some calcium carbonate into the water sample, (it won't dissolve) and then bubble carbon dioxide gas through the cloudy water from a soda stream apparatus or whatever you have available, until the chalk dissolves up (as calcium hydrogen carbonate). Adding calcium carbonate to half a bottle of fresh mineral water and shaking should do the trick too. Appendix 1 contains a sample calculation which will enable you to maintain some control over the amount of hardness which is so achieved.

Hardening Water. A cautionary tale.

There are some seemingly scholarly books on home-brewing which give comprehensive tables on how much of what salt to add to water in order to harden it. The only problem is that home brewers without the confidence of a scientific training will shy from the necessary calculations and quite rightly so, for the wrong addition of certain salts could land you in all sorts of trouble, especially as some salts have powerful laxative properties. Even those of us with the skill and enthusiasm to mix extra ingredients into our water will find that exact dosing of the salts is not easy. I will give you one example which illustrates the point.

As an approximation one book says that the addition of one level teaspoon of the salt magnesium sulphate to 5 gallons of water will add 50 ppm calcium ions and 125 ppm sulphate ions, assuming a standard medicinal teaspoon of 5 cm^3 capacity. Now magnesium sulphate is an "intestinal purgative", as the text books say and is readily soluble in water, which means if you put too much in it will dissolve up and you won't know until it is too late. Magnesium sulphate occurs naturally in Stassfurt as the mono-hydrate $MgSO_4.H_2O$ and in Epsom as the hepta-hydrate $MgSO_4.7H_2O$. The figures quoted in the learned treatise mentioned are for Epsom salts but if you inadvertently purchase the mono-hydrate which is chemically identical, just containing less water, you will actually add 1.7 times the expected amount by following the instructions given!

The same text states that the addition of one teaspoon of calcium carbonate will increase the calcium ion concentration by 30ppm when added to 5 gallons of water. This is the same as 30 mg/l. Now the solubility of calcium carbonate is only 13 mg/l at room temperature (hence the White Cliffs are still at Dover after 92 million years) and so the most you can increase the calcium ion concentration using calcium carbonate, is 5 mg/l. I believe that the unsuspecting author had been confused by the annoying habit of water analysis sheets of quoting temporary hardness in "ppm carbonate", which is what precipitates out, not what is dissolved up. Calcium hydrogen carbonate however doesn't exist as the dry salt and so cannot be added by the teaspoon. The water board chemists know what they're talking about but do we? If in doubt, use your water as it comes out of the tap and don't mess about with it.

As a rule of thumb it is sufficient to remember that soft water is usually satisfactory for pale, highly hopped beers and hard water makes good darker exemplars.

The table of famous brewing waters in appendix 1 reveals that Munich, Dortmund and Vienna should be known for moderately hopped dark beers while Pilsen is noted for a very pale but highly hopped beverage. The brewery in Lingen made excellent slightly darkened moderately hopped strong ales. Its output was small but then so was my cellar.

"The first and foremost material for brewing is water that one can drink, wet and cold which taketh unto itself the qualities and properties of the Things with which it is mixed and made up or with which it is decocted or boiled. For if it is cooked with cold adjuncts so it taketh cold properties and if it is cooked with warm adjuncts so it taketh warm properties and loseth and leaveth its own Nature."

That is how, after thirteen pages praising God and the King, Heinrich Knaust, Doctor and Royal and Crowned Poet Laureate, advised his readers on St. Anthony's Day in 1575 to choose their brewing water, and we should worry about the sulphate ion concentration? Knaust will have been highly motivated to make good beer. Fools and failures were not lightly tolerated in his day. In the reign of William I, the ducking stool was ordered for bad ale (malam cerevisiam faciens).

Acidity, Alkalinity and pH of the Water.

As has been previously stated, enzymes are biological catalysts which are responsible for breaking down the large starch molecules into dextrines and maltose and then for dispatching the latter, with the help of fermentation, as ethanol (an alcohol) and carbon dioxide. When considering the function of enzymes it is useful to have some appreciation of how they work. A simple but helpful model is to imagine them as keys. Certain keys have the correct shape to open certain locks, and certain molecules have the correct shape and chemical properties to fit into a starch molecule, open it up, be removed and then be available for use on another part of the same, or different molecule to "open" it up. Such molecular "keys," are called enzymes and the "opening up", is really breaking the large molecule down into smaller parts, in this case breaking the polysaccharide starch down into the disaccharide maltose. The processes involved and the exact nature of enzymes are very complicated and is only over-shadowed by the complexity of the manifold biological processes which, all things being equal, the enzymes get right every time they are called upon.

All this means that enzymes are very smart molecules, but in order to have just the right shape to go to work on, they feel they are entitled to have just the right conditions. They like it warm, but not too hot or their structure may be changed irreversibly. If it is too cold then they will work too slowly and the wort is at the mercy of other microbes which will conspire to turn it into something other than beer. They are a little bit sensitive about the pH (measure of acidity or alkalinity) of the mash or fermentation, but will generally put up with everything except extremes. Again it must be said that only the commercial brewery is interested in optimising every step in the process and we are under no pressure to achieve exactly the right temperature and pH. Variations in mashing temperature and pH will result in a variation in the product for we alter the emphasis in the miriad of reactions taking place and thus the nature of the final beer. It is by no means inevitable that altering the brewing conditions slightly and thus the nature of the beer, will lower the quality. Exact control of brewing conditions is quite a new phenomenon and a yearning for a standardised product has no place in historical brewing. It is also common practice for home-brewers to start a brew one day and then finish it the next, simply because inconveniences such as earning a living force him or her to spread over 24 hours what the professional does in two.

What experience has shown is that a good brew will usually have had a certain mash pH and temperature. The latter is easily controlled by adding hot or cold water, and the action of the malt in water should give the mash the correct slightly acidic conditions without us having to interfere. If it doesn't then your recipe is probably incompatible with the water at your disposal and it is worth knowing how to ascertain this.

pH.

Students of brewing should remember the relative importance of water and acidity. Get the water right and the acidity will look after itself. Given the chance, biological systems almost invariably create the conditions which they require, redressing imbalances themselves. The brewer who tries to use external forces to regulate the acidity of his mash or fermentation will end up in a pickle.

The term "acidity", refers to the hydrogen ion concentration in the water. Even the purest water dissociates into hydrogen ions albeit only slightly. The concentration is actually 10^{-7} mols/l and if you take the negative logarithm of that you get the number 7. This explains the name pH, *power* to which the *Hydrogen* ion concentration is raised. Remember pure water is neutral and is given the pH value 7. Strong dilute acid will have a value of less than 2 and a strong alkali a value between 11-14. Although the pH scale runs for practical purposes from 1-14, we never have to deal in the kitchen with acids stronger than vinegar (pH 3) or alkalis stronger than baking powder (pH 8-9 when in solution).

Many natural and synthetic coloured substances change colour when the hydrogen ion concentration or acidity is altered and so we have an easy way of determining the pH of our mash or fermentation liquor. One can buy strips of filter paper which have been soaked in a combination of colours, each of which reveals itself at a specific pH. The most common of these so called "indicator papers" is the Universal Indicator, the scale of which is approximately described below.

pH-Scale Number	Type of Solution	Indicator Colour
1-3	strong acid	red
4-6	weak acid	orange to straw
7	neutral	green
8 & 9	weak alkali	green/blue
10-14	strong alkali	dark blue to purple

The brewing process only involves pH-values between about 4 and 8 and so one best buys a special indicator paper which covers that range, but does so with greater accuracy than a full range indicator. Whatever type of paper is purchased, it always comes with a colour scale so measurements are easily made. One problem though is that worts are rarely themselves colourless, so pH-papers must be used with discretion. If in doubt, don't interfere.

When a new recipe is tried the following should be taken into consideration.

1) Choose your recipe bearing in mind the water at your disposal. The recipes given in this book give an indication of the types of water most suitable.

2) There are only two ways of naturally regulating the pH of a mash.
   -remove the temporary hardness.
   -add dark malt.

3) Temporary hard water containing a lot of carbonate hardness will have a pH of about 7.8.

4) The hydrogen carbonate can be removed from temporary hard water by boiling for several minutes and this should give a pH closer to 7.

5) The malt with which you mash should bring the pH down to about 5.2-5.5 which is the optimum for the enzymes.

6) The addition of dark malt to temporary hard water also brings the pH down thus removing the necessity of boiling the water in order to achieve a pH of 5.2 for the mash. More than 20% dark malts shouldn't be used unless a distinctive dark malt flavour is required.

7) During fermentation the pH should drop to about 4.

8) If the above optimum pH-values cannot be observed, plough on regardless and finish the brew. If you are dissatisfied with the product try a different recipe next time.

9) If an indicator paper is available then check the pH at the various stages. Don't worry too much about the pH because malting and brewing are such elegant processes that they create their own ideal conditions for each stage of the beer making. The occasional check is worthwhile so that one can be sure that all is well.

Spicing the Beer.

"The manifold virtues in Hops (cleansing and opening the body, purging the blood, calming the nerves and curing insomnia etc.) do manifestly argue the holesomeness of Beere above Ale, for the Hops make it a Phisicall drinke to keep the body in health, than an ordinarie drinke for the quenching of our thirst."

Thus Gerard in 1597 alludes to the battle of tastes which raged between ale, spiced with Bog Myrtle, Yarrow and Ground Ivy and the newer beer, spiced with hops. Since the arrival of hops for flavouring beer the ale drinker had shown considerable consumer resistance. The word "beer", in the English language is, as previously hinted, reputed to be a compromise to pacify the ale drinker who wanted to be sure that he wasn't getting the new fangled hopped beer when he ordered a drink. The taste of hops was not initially highly rated by the average English ale drinker but he seems to have got used to it, perhaps because storing beer had always been a problem and hopped beer kept better than the ales.

As already stated, the hop is thought to have arrived in England during the

16th century with the Dutch emigrants who quickly set up hop gardens in Kent, Worcestershire and Sussex but hops may have been in use in England before this time. Certainly we know that the Grout was being replaced in Germany with hops by the 8th century and possibly before. The Benedictine Monks in the Kloster Freising were systematically cultivating hops for their beer by that time. Equally certain is that the Grut was alive and well in Germany and the Low Countries as late as the 15th century and the herbal beers described in Chapter 10 date from that time.

The exact nature of very early Grouts can only be guessed at. Every household had their secret tip, a tradition which is still common among brewers, and some herbs may have disappeared from our everyday vegetation and are thus difficult for us to characterise. The recipe for a Mum ale recorded in the chapter on historical beers, contains information on a particular Grout. It was made up from cardus benedictus, rosa solis, itself a mixture of herbs such as burnet, betony, marjoram, avens, penny royal, elder flowers and wild thyme. Grigson quotes an ale grout from the 1548 edition of Cogan's "Haven of Health". The grout itself was known as Rosa Solis and this version was a mixture of equal parts of rosemary, sage, thyme, chamomile, marjoram, mint, avens, fennel, dill, pelletory, lavender, hyssop, roses and spices. If the exact mixtures depended on the locality, then across borders totally different herbs were used. In England nettle beer was common but due to the slightly salty taste it seems not to have been popular. The nettle is related to the hop and the tasty tips are certainly plentiful in early summer. Dandelion beer is reported to have been drunk in labouring communities until quite recently as its diuretic properties were valued by men who needed to drink a lot because of physical exertion. Nettle beer enjoys the same reputation. Rosemary was a common herb for spicing and medicinal purposes and judging by the extensive plantations of this bush in some English country gardens, such as that adjoining Anne Hathaway's cottage, this lovely herb must have been used in huge quantities. Alecost or costmary is known as an ale spice by the Oxford Dictionary but not mentioned in detail by Grigson. This aster (*chrysanthemum balsamita*) has a long history of cultivation for flavouring ale, in this country and abroad.

Hops

Hops originated in Asia and their use for spicing beer came to us via Eastern Europe.

As the family tree shows, the hop is a distant relative of the stinging nettle and cannabis. This may explain the relaxing effect which hops have, for they

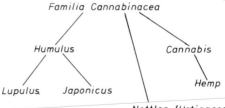

Familia Cannabinacea

Humulus   Cannabis

Lupulus   Japonicus   Hemp

Nettles (Urticaceae caceae)

have been used as a herb against insomnia since their earliest mention in the literature. In England it is also common practice during the hop harvest for Londoners, gypsies, students, etc. to take a cheap working holiday in Kent and help with the picking. Anyone who has picked hops will tell you of the marvellous time they had doing it and in what a happy mood they were after only a few minutes among the twines. I'm sure this has something to do with the mild narcotic quality of this delightful plant. Monckton records this description of nineteenth century hop-pickers.

"But if the pickers are merry and lighthearted on their way to the fields, with empty pockets, what are they on their return, after work is over and wages paid? Everything then is the height of merriment, and of such an uproarious kind as the people of the East End delight in. Young men and girls, invigorated by their sojourn in the bracing country air, alike garland themselves with hops, and decorate themselves with gay ribbons. Laughing, dancing and singing they hurry to the station or along the road to London".

Apparently local people barred their doors and windows and the railway companies put on extra staff to deal with the high life that was to be expected.

The hop also has a place in folklore. Along with the animals, who are supposed to receive the gift of speech late on Christmas Eve, the hop is believed to turn green in the same night. It has always had a chequered history, sometimes harvesting great praise as a cure-all, including insomnia, hysteria, indigestion, hypochondria, gout, aphrodisiac and preventer of premature ejaculation, blood purifier and aid to the complexion. But then again the 16th century writer Boorde considered it a natural drink for the Dutch but likely to cause fatness and an inflated belly in an Englishman. What does the friendly hop have to do with wolves or foxes? Humulus is a latinized version of the northern word for hop and lupulus because the Romans saw it as a parasite, living among and choking more useful plants; a wolf in sheep's clothing?

Hop
Humulus lupulus

Only the female flower of Humulus Lupulus is used for spicing beer. German growers go to the trouble of exterminating the male plant because they consider that the female flower in seed has a poorer percentage taste component than the unfertilised flower. The seeds are also alleged to disturb the clarification process of a bottom fermenter.

The hop is a mighty grower and in order to reach its height of 5-7 m (this need not be entirely vertical growth) it must manage up to 15 cm per day, which is just as well for the young shoots are highly prized by birds who in my garden are happy to fight the unequal battle with this prolific perennial.

The hop prefers shade early in the year, (March to May) and then to grow into the light. The first shoots, which appear in March, are popular in Swabia (South West Germany) where they are picked and cooked in lightly salted water, rather like asparagus. They are reputed to have replaced asparagus during lean times, and although Gerard found the shoots "more toothsome than nourishing", Grigson is evidently not even impressed with the quality of their "toothsomeness", never mind their nourishment. The recipes which I have from Swabia don't sound too bad at all and as I hope that every house-brewer will have a hop plant in his garden, I give a cross section of the hop's other uses in the kitchen in appendix 2.

Strains of Hop.

There are different varieties of humulus lupulus, which are all strains of the original Asian import. The most sought after these days are the Hallertauer which have their home in Bavaria, but are now grown throughout beer making lands. The taste is undoubtedly the best of any sort and a really top quality Hallertauer will make a beer as you have never tasted and blended with the alcohol have you doing things you never done. Those grown in Germany have no seeds in the flower which means that because the dried flower is very light and the seed relatively heavy, you get much more hop for your money. Hallertauer can be used in any type of beer although it is most at home in the South German dark beers.

Saaz comes from Bohemia in North Eastern Czechoslovakia which is also the origin of Pils. Saaz are the very apex of hop flavour for light beers.

My praise of the continental types should not be interpreted as hostility to the English varieties. Goldings give the typical flavour required for light ales and bitters, but contain plenty of seeds in the flowers, (which provides me with an excuse for some of my beers not clearing perfectly) and if you are thinking of your garden, are rather prone to blight (called "wilt", in the trade) and aren't heavy croppers.

Fuggle is worth using just for the name but has a strong flavour which may not suit every taste. They can be used in weakly hopped beers such as mild ales, stouts etc.

Northern Brewer is a harsh hop and 60 g for a 30l brew is considered enough in stouts and dark ales.

Bullion comes from across the Atlantic and has a distinctive flavour.

Growing your own hops.

"Because it is easy to grow, so they should be in every garden; every landowner should devote a small area to them, sufficiently large to allow in a good hop year enough hops to be grown for his own house brewery and maybe more that he can earn himself some thalers through their sale."

(Johann Gottfried Hahn, 1804)

If you grow your own, which Hahn definitely advises, you will need adequate support for the vine and about 2 m around the roots for growth. The roots, although prolific, don't disturb small shallow root flowers but may give shrubs a hard time. Hop-vines don't like a windy position and although they are decorative in summer, don't enhance much in winter, when the growth has died back and only the dried foliage is left. The support need not be a problem as the hop twines do not damage their hosts and I let mine grow through and along a hawthorn hedge. This has an added advantage of making me cut the hedge in order to harvest them.

The hop farmer grows them up wires 7 m in height around which they twine in a clockwise direction, using the hairs on their stems to hang on. The wires are lowered from the long poles for the harvest in late August or September and the growth dies back completely for winter. If you wish to achieve 6-7 m vertical growth then a support on a protected house wall will be needed.

Hops like a mild clay or marl soil with plenty of humus and tolerably well drained. They are heavy feeders when producing the flowers and professional growers apply liquid nitrate dressings during this time. One can obtain the 3-5 year old roots from nursery men or hop growers and these should be planted about 1.25 m apart at a depth of 12 cm in heavily dressed troughs. 8-10 shoots will soon appear and of these 2-3 are tied to the support, the others being picked and used for the hop shoot recipes described in appendix 2. The rows will soon grow over with weeds as the hop vines offer little competition at ground level. Thus they will need frequent hoeing and heaping around the base of the plant.

The harvest during the first year is usually relatively modest, but thereafter improves dramatically. 2 kg/vine was achieved (wet weight) in 1951 which, as these figures pre-date extensive mineral fertilizer use, are relevant to the small hop garden. The fresh flowers contain 80% water which is reduced to 12% during the drying process. Thus 2 kg/vine becomes a more modest 455 g of usable dry substance, which, depending on how strongly the beer is to be hopped, will suffice for 4 to 6 brews of 20l. Two heavy cropping vines should keep moderate drinkers going from one hop harvest to the next.

The easiest way to obtain fresh hops is to take a country walk in early autumn for you should find wild hops in profusion, climbing out the hedgerow and hanging on to available trees. The hedgerows on the A1 at Biggleswade or north of Peterborough have enough wild hops to keep many home brewers going but a quick detour down a quiet country lane provides much more pleasant picking. I have spotted excellent wild hops in hedgerows in Surrey, Sussex, Kent, and East Anglia, but not in the Northern Counties. This cannot be due to the inclement weather of the North as I have also picked good hops in the Emsland, which must be the draughtiest most inhospitable flatland in North Europe.

The Triangular Bavarian Driers use only air circulation to dry the hops.

Only pick the female flowers. These appear after the tiny star shaped males have died back. They come out of the same stem join as the leaves and are unmistakably cone shaped. In your own hop garden you may want to prevent the female flowers from producing seeds and this is best done by destroying the male flowers as soon as they appear. Even better is to destroy the male plants but this is easier said than done. Having once identified the male vine it is no easy matter to follow it back to the root through the maze of twines. If there are wild hops growing nearby then killing the male plant is a lost cause anyway.

Some skill is required in deciding when to pick for the flowers should not be fully mature and without experience it is difficult to avoid being wise only after the event. Hahn insists that the only time to pick is the right time. Too early or too late just won't do, so I wait until the first flowers show a hint of brown. These I reject, but immediately harvest all others. In fact the unripe flowers are green, those ready for picking, yellow and the spent cones have skirts of brown. If at all possible one should never harvest wet flowers. If the harvest is a good one then the flowers are unpleasantly oily and have a strong distinctive aroma. The real skill now is required for the drying of the flowers. Only when dry will the hops keep and if they are not to lose too much of their quality and flavour, drying must be carried out immediately.

Drying the hops.

The triangular drying sheds shown in the picture of 19th century hop driers made maximum use of the sun's warmth. Huge ventilator openings can be seen on the roof and it is fair to assume that the shed shown had three floors. Note also that the windows are well shuttered to keep out the light. This simple oast house applied on a large scale the traditional method of drying herbs which had been known for aeons when one hung the freshly picked leaves or flowers in small bunches in an airy loft void. Even the late summer sun playing on such long dark roofs was enough to raise the temperature under the slates to around 30°C which is about the optimum for drying. In a cool autumn, or in a loft which didn't warm sufficiently, the hops were spread in a single layer and turned every day. As the drying proceeded they were heaped into ever thicker layers, ending finally as a single mound of hops.

The amateur hop grower should modify the old German method for drying his harvest. Before the current use of roofing felt became general, any house in a fairly exposed position had a good draft in a warm loft and hence one could clear a space in autumn and dry without problems. Good ventilation is most important and some modern domestic lofts may be a bit short of air but even so any available windows should be shut in damp weather and overnight. Light must be excluded at all times, which can make the use of windows for ventilation difficult. The Bavarian drying sheds had loosely fitting wood or slate shingle on the roof, which allowed a good passage of air. In a very poor autumn wet air may have to be excluded and then drying could last into November.

German hop farmers considered November to be the earliest date the hops can be filled into sacks but I have found no temperature records for the drying floors used during the last century when this method was common. Hahn gives a

The English Oast House with a sack ready for treading.

useful tip for telling when the hops are dry enough:- as the stalks on the flower become so brittle that they break as against flexing when bent.

The English Oast House contrived to achieve the same effect as the triangular Bavarian sheds but didn't rely too heavily on a sunny September. Hot air from convectors passes up through the bed of hops, which may be as deep as 3 feet. The cowl at the top turns into the wind thus leaving reduced pressure behind the cowl, causing air to be drawn up through the hop bed. There are also trap doors between the various floors to allow ventilation to be reduced on very windy days.

When the hops are dry, they are rammed into cylindrical sacks using a heavy press, both of which are visible in the picture. Ernest Shepard, the illustrator of "Wind in the Willows", and "Winnie the Pooh", left a delightful description of a 19th century hop harvest, oast house and "Dan".

"The oast house was a round building with a pointed roof and ladders leading to the top. It was divided into floors. The hops were dried by being spread on a sort of wire frame. A man with a wooden rake kept turning them over and over. Down below some small fires were burning with a blue flame; these were being fed with some yellow stuff which the man, on being questioned, said was sulphur. It made my throat tingle. Presently, when the hops were dry enough, they were gathered up and taken to another floor. This had a round hole in the middle, with a great long sack fixed in it. 'We calls that the pocket,' said the man. 'An' you watch how we presses 'em. Dan!' he called, 'are 'e ready?' Dan had a very old felt hat with a wide brim, which he turned down so that you could only see the lower part of his face. Then they tipped some hops into the long sack and Dan lowered himself in after them, slowly disappearing, until only the top of his hat could be seen. ' 'e does the treadin',' explained the man and Dan began to tread, working round and round while more hops were poured over his head.

Gradually Dan began to reappear, very unkempt and dusty: first his hat, then his shoulders: as more hops were poured in he rose higher and higher".

If the easiest method for drying is to spread the hop flowers in an airy loft in thin layers this presupposes that a loft of sufficient surface area and cleanliness is available and you have a good surface of south facing roof, capable of realising a temperature of 30°C or more inside the loft. Ideally, the hops should be laid on wire mesh so that air can pass through the bed from all directions. Should you be able to meet these constraints then before starting the drying process, weigh a large sample of the hops, say 1 kg. Of this 1 kg, 800 g are water and 200 g hop substance. The water is removed until this 200 g hop substance becomes 88% of the mass. In this dried state the total mass, including the 12% water is 227 g.

As soon as this mass reduction has been reached, the dried hops are wrapped in aluminium foil and kept in a cool place, preferably the freezer. Only use plastic bags if you have room in the freezer because the essential volatile constituents will diffuse through thin plastic films in no time at all at room temperature!! Ramming the dried hops into cloth sacks so that no air can pass through may be the traditional method of storing, but not easily achieved in a modern kitchen.

If like me you have no loft suitable at your disposal, you will have to construct a drier. Such methods are problematic but with patience success will come. Large cardboard boxes and hair dryers are tempting propositions. Don't bother! The air velocity up through the box must be roughly measured by placing the hops in the box and holding them loosely in place by sandwiching them between two layers of fine chicken wire. The box has to be then turned on its side and the hair dryer, which has been entered through the base of the box started. The time taken for a large feather or something similar to travel a measured metre distance within the box is measured. Now comes the tricky part. Burgess in his comprehensive work on hop production, recommends the following temperatures and air velocities for drying hops.

Air velocity	Air Temperature
3 m/min	33°C.
8 m/min	45°C.
13 m/min	55°C.

If the feather velocity falls outside the above values given by Burgess, the air velocity can be speeded up by reducing the thickness of the hop bed or slowed down by shutting the lid of the box a little. Assuming you achieve a value between 3-13 m/min you now have to adjust the temperature to suit and doing this without upsetting the air velocity is not easy. The temperature can only be regulated by the distance of the hair dryer from the inlet point in the box. A further problem is that at a velocity of 13 m/min and temperature of 55°C, four hours drying time may be needed. Four hours is a running time for which no domestic hair dryer was constructed. When the temperature of the inlet and outlet air is the same, the hops are dry. The above mentioned problems can be solved with perseverance, but not with hair dryers. An oven can be easily constructed, heated with a domestic fan heater and the temperature controlled with a "Burst fire/proportional temperature controller". This is described in appendix 6.

Far easier is to hope for a hot day and construct some chicken wire trays which, with their edges bent upwards, will stack on each other. The edges need to allow for about 3 cm depth of hop cones and 6 cm air space between hop cone layers. Stack the trays in a darkened shed or in an airing cupboard. If the temperature of your drying cabinet is about 30°C then circulate the air within the cabinet with a fan heater without the elements switched on. A potting shed in the sun is preferable as the whole shed becomes the drying cabinet and if it is too cool then the fan heater can be adjusted to safely blow hot air over the hop trays.

If a glass house or conservatory is available then darken a small area off using black bin liners. If you are not in a hurry and it is of little consequence if the hops are dry in four hours or four weeks then simply spread the cones thinly in a dark airy place and forget them for a few days.

A sample of the hops must be weighed before starting the drying so that you know when the necessary weight reduction has been achieved and the approximate water content can be estimated.

Above all remember that there is no magic to drying hops! When in doubt think of those German monks in Freising in the eighth century without as much as a thermometer at their disposal.

If you visit a hop growing area of the country, do buy a few pounds of some of the different varieties. I have always found hop merchants most helpful about supplying even small quantities. Good home-brew shops can buy hops in bulk and bag up a large quantity for you (say 5 lbs) before they are stacked on light warm display shelves. Hops purchased in this way are of quality and price to boot, which should shame some famous supermarket chains.

Testing Hop Quality.

Good quality dried hop cones feel oily, unpleasantly sticky and release an almost anaesthetizing aroma. The stickiness is sufficient to cause a crushed flower to adhere as a ball to the palm of the hand. The seeds may still be intact inside the flower, but should fall out easily. The petals however should remain attached to the flower stem and the flowers should not disintegrate when handled. The seeds are hard but when crushed form a yellow flour like powder. Try these tests on some of the home-brew shop hops which are kept loosely packed in plastic bags at temperatures in excess of 20°C and in bright light. Such samples on sale in supermarkets should be avoided at all cost. The dried hops cannot tolerate being kept in the light, warmth or loosely in perforated plastic bags. The contents of these bags are always dry, non sticky, and brittle and have done more to bring home-brewing into disrepute than anything else. Hahn had the same complaint nearly 200 years ago and wrote "nothing has brought house-brewing into disrepute more than the disgraceful hops being employed". He recommended the use of surrogates such as buckbean if decent hops were not available (see Chapter 10).

These days one reckons on about 10-40 g hops per 5l beer, but in past centuries 3-5 times these quantities were common. This may reveal a shift in taste, or perhaps the large quantities were thought to preserve better the often unhygienically prepared beer. I suspect though that the problems of storing hops from one year to the next meant that some very poor cones were used and in order to try and make up for the missing oils and taste components, quantity instead of quality was the by-word. It is possible to compensate for poor hops by using more but the result is never the same as a beer made with good quality ingredients.

Old hops are aggravating but wild hops can be an absolute disaster and make the beer taste like medicine. If you grow your own hops or dry wild hops, always test them carefully by making an ale from a small sample of the dried product. Included in the recipe section is a North German method employed for making a quick beer in Schleswig Holstein during the 17th century. This recipe is close to the 18th century "Ale on a Small Scale", method which is included under the English recipes. Either of these methods is suitable for quickly testing some hops. The German beer employs wheat and will have its own unique, slightly sour taste so be careful not to blame the hops for the intrinsic qualities of this type of beer.

Hop Extracts.

"Double, double toil and trouble;
Fire burn, and cauldron bubble."

(Macbeth's witches.)

Many breweries no longer use dried hops but hop extract. The extract is made by running hot solvent through the hop cones and thereby extracting the organic material. Excess solvent is then evaporated to leave a thick pasty dark green extract or powder which may be pelleted. The extracts are more concentrated weight for weight than the dried hops conventionally used. Using extracts has many advantages:

1) One works with smaller quantities. This is not such an advantage in terms of weight even though the extract weighs less than the equivalent dried hops, but in volume. The dried hops are rammed into sacks in order to try and reduce the bulk problem and loss of fragrance but even so the extract demands a fraction of the storage volume and can be kept longer without detriment to the quality.

2) Most organic substances are steam volatile. This means that during the cooking of the hops in the wort, useful hop flavouring is being boiled off with the steam. Some brewers believe that harmful substances are removed from the hops in this way and that a minimum boiling time is essential. Dr. Knaust in 1575 was most worried about lack of cooking of the wort. He wrote, "Many beers are properly and healthily cooked, and many right badly, either due to a wood shortage, or because the brewmaster and his apprentices do not pay diligent attention and see that everything is done properly and due attention done to all things.

Many beers are coarsely hopped especially when they are not adequately cooked or sozzled. Such beers damage the stomach, cause digestive problems, cause chills in the kidneys, bladder and urethra."

What we don't know is how many of these fearful complaints were caused by the wort not being properly sterilised through too shorter boiling. I doubt that such illnesses can all be laid at the door of inadequately cooked hops. Since then it has been generally accepted that the wort must be sterile and boiled for at least one hour to clear it of suspended particles. The hops are added in portions to the wort during the duration of the boiling, no portion being boiled for less than 15 minutes. That is the minimum time required for the hop oils to isomerise and form the molecules which spice the beer.

By adding the hops gradually during the boiling of the wort, we achieve a full range of hop components by replacing those most quickly boiled off. Hop extracts can be most easily and accurately dosed for this purpose thus minimising the amount of organic oils lost by steam distillation.

3) Solvent extraction of the hop oils reduces loss of these oils, which normally occurs during storage as the dried pellets or thick concentrate may be sealed in metal containers and kept almost indefinitely.

Home brewers still prefer boiling up the dried cones. Despite all, the beer is better, and it looks and feels the part. Some people however find the smell of the hops cooking in the wort quite disgusting. One can of course only pity them. Hops, like garlic, are above earthly criticism!

Yeast.

"Only in the most extreme emergency should one attempt to make one's own yeast. The Persians put a spoonful of crushed peas in a little boiling water which is left overnight in a warm place. In the morning a froth will reveal itself on the top which has all the properties of a good yeast."

(Hahn 1804.)

We can now purchase so many reliable yeast strains from the home-brew shop that it would be foolish to risk our valuable brew by using some cultivated wild yeast. Hahn also gives recipes for making yeast from wheat flour and interestingly enough similar methods are still used by German bakers to make *Sauerteig*, which is the raising agent for many of the faintly sour continental rye breads. If such methods are reliable enough for bakers they could be of more than historical interest for the inquisitive brewer. I have concocted the following recipe using Hahn's scanty description and a modern baker's recipe. So for the really brave, or just for the historical record, here is how one makes yeast.

Ingredients.

> Hop flavouring
> Water 200 ml
> Wheat flour 200 g
> Pinch of salt

Mix all the ingredients in luke warm water to form a thick porridge. Cover with a cloth and stand for 5-6 days at about 25°C.

or

> Hop flavouring
> Wheat flour 200 g
> Butter milk 200 ml
> Pinch of salt
> Tablespoon sugar or honey

Mix the ingredients to form a porridge and leave for 5-6 days at 25°C.

These yeast surrogates will certainly have a slightly sour flavour, and perhaps impart it to the first brew from such a strain as the fermentation will not be caused by pure yeast but is the work of wild yeast present in the flour and the lactobacilli bacteria. The latter changes carbon compounds such as glucose (the building block for starch) into lactic acid (present in sour milk) and vinegar. As only half the amount of yeast so prepared was added to the fermentation tub, the sour taste became diluted and with it the problem. The other half was kept until the next brew and then 24 hours before it was needed, freshened up by whisking in half the ingredient quantity. The yeast strain could thus be started but if the brew was successful, an excess of yeast would be available for future brews. In this way successive brews enhanced the yeast fermentation at the expense of lactobacilli fermentation. It is worth asking of course if the sour taste of the lactobacilli fermentation wasn't sought after in much the same way as the sour taste of the continental rye breads? Anyone for a spoonful of yoghurt in their beer?

If the next brew was to be more than one week hence, then the yeast slurry was freshened every seven days. If you manage to develop a good strain with this method then you are worthy of the Croix de Guerre of home-brewing for the exact nature of a yeast strain is still one of the most cherished and fiercely protected secrets of any brewery.

The object of adding the yeast is to convert the sugar to alcohol and carbon dioxide and nowadays there are two yeast strains commonly used by brewers. Hahn warned severely about using bottom fermenting yeast, which is strange because bottom fermenters are now used almost exclusively on the Continent. Only forty years after Hahn, other writers such as Müller extolled the virtues of bottom fermenting. Hahn's objection may have been simply old fashioned prejudice.

There are two types of fermentation which take place alongside each other and whilst we cannot eliminate one or other, we can, by altering the conditions, favour one type at the expense of the other. In fact the reaction favoured by the bottom fermenters produces a purer product.

In the presence of air, or more accurately, atmospheric oxygen, the yeast uses the sugar as an energy source and with the oxygen, ferments to produce some alcohol, quite a lot of carbon dioxide and at the same time, reproduce. This aerobic fermentation takes place best at the surface of the beer, where there is enough oxygen and is thus favoured by the lower density top fermenting yeasts of the Saccharomyces Cerevisiae family, which float on the top of the wort. In pre-industrial society, yeasts were frequently very suspect, and by allowing aerobic fermentation, one was in fact breeding one's own yeast. Because this was being done in a "beer medium", the reproduction of the good beer yeast cells was favoured and the other "wild" cells were less successful at reproducing. A form of cell selection took place.

Yeasts of the Saccharomyces Carlsbergensis strain ferment at the bottom of the tub and as there is less available oxygen in the wort, "anaerobic", fermentation proceeds with the consequent conversion of the sugar into mainly alcohol, some carbon dioxide and correspondingly less cell reproduction. Seen from a purely theoretical standpoint, the brewer should favour the bottom fermenters as less sugar is wasted producing carbon dioxide and yeast cells. He does tie up capital and equipment though as their progress is favoured by lower temperatures and so fermentation takes longer. Bottom fermenters are used nearly exclusively in every country except the U.K. If you do experiment with your own yeast strains, then do remember that the microbes produced under anaerobic or aerobic conditions can pose a considerable health risk. Be guided by your nose and common sense. The ability of bottom fermenters to be able to work at low temperatures means the cool wort is under less attack from unwanted microbes.

Coupled with the fact that Continental beers are also mashed differently we can see why lager beers have their own quality. The low temperatures allow the beer to hold far greater amounts of dissolved carbon dioxide gas and favour a purer fermentation process. The former explains the gassy nature of lagers, (and that oh so important head which the Germans must have) compared to healthy, nutritional but flat English beers.

Loosing one's yeast strain has always been one of the greatest and most intractable disasters which could beset a brewer. Nowadays breweries keep reserve stocks of their particular yeast in fridges to which only the brewmaster has access. A sample is also often kept at the laboratories of a specialist yeast manufacturer. If a brew does go wrong and has to be destroyed then the brewery can be sure it will not loose its own particular strain. One wouldn't expect present day breweries to have problems with their beer hygiene. The fermentation vats are kept scrupulously clean and the fermentation process takes place in sterile rooms to which only a few workers are allowed access. Thus the excess yeast from one brew can be ladled off and added to the next wort. Breweries still produce more yeast than they can use themselves and traditionally they supplied bakers with their daily requirement as well as other brewers, who for one reason or another had not brewed recently and lost their own supply. In some parts of the country it was an offence for brewers to refuse a customer a supply of yeast and in a case quoted by Monckton from the 15th century, it appears they were required by law to supply enough yeast to brew from a quarter of malt for not more than a farthing. Without such regulations, a brewer would have been able to put his competitors out of business.

Another reason for using bottom fermenting yeasts which will continue to work at low temperatures is that the yeast enzymes continue to operate during the cool storage period which beers undergo these days. Beers begin to become really clear when the yeast has finished all activity and there is no usable nourishment left in the beer for the yeast. Once the yeast activity has ceased, the liquid clears more completely at lower temperatures. One must set against this that the more dissolved solute which is precipitated out of a cold liquid, the less nourishment is left in the beer for us to drink. This perverse desire for a totally clear beer has become something of an anathema for good brewing but the home-brewer is in a position to ignore the stupidity of his commercial colleagues. Not only do Continental brewers ferment at low temperatures to encourage the complete settling out of the yeast after fermentation, but they then filter the beer through fine sand (Kieselgur) in order to remove even the slightest trace of a yeast cell. This filtering removes a lot of colour as well as proteins from the beer which have precipitated out at the low temperature. This means that lager drinkers pay more for a far less substantial drink. Every German health food shop sells the same yeast at inflated prices, for being rich in vitamin B it is a very beneficial health adjunct. Provided that the residual yeast, starch and proteins are not present in too greater quantities in beer, the problem of haze is only optical, for the taste of the beer is not altered for the worse by the presence of suspended solids. We must at all costs resist the temptation to try and achieve the clarity which modern brewers have convinced the drinking public they require. English brewers are well on the way to having us believe that we prefer a very pale tasteless imitation of what passes for continental beer, served at ridiculously low temperatures and high prices. Have nothing of it! The "lager market", didn't exist in the U.K. and had to be created by advertising and you may be sure it wasn't for the benefit of the consumer.

The historical evidence is that the clarity of beer seems to have become important with the use of glass drinking vessels during the 19th century. Stoneware, pewter, wood and leather were the traditional materials for a beer mug and beer still tastes best from a cool stone pot. Due to storage problems it was common to drink beer within a few days of fermentation, when it certainly wasn't clear and several such recipes are contained in the chapters on early beers.

Bottom fermenting of beer seems to have started in a very limited way in Germany in the 13th century but without refrigeration did not come into its own until the late 19th century. Before such technology was available, these beers could only be made with the help of cool caves. The Paulaner Brauerei in Munich still uses a huge cave in the Nockerberg to make and serve their Lent fast beer Salvator. The modern home brewer is unlikely to get away with taking the fridge over for eight weeks in order to make lager but as the temperature required is between 0-10°C, brewing in a shed in the winter months is obviously favourite.

Like the commercial brewer you will always have an excess of yeast in the bottom of a fermenting tub and it can be worth keeping this as a starter for the next brew, especially if you have been fortunate enough to get a sample of fresh brewers' yeast from your local brewery. Such fresh samples are infinitely better than anything you can purchase in the way of dried yeasts. The following method for preserving a yeast sample for the next brew I also owe to Hahn, who points out that in the 18th century losing your yeast strain was even worse than letting the fire go out. Some 17th century recipes for re-creating a yeast include ingredients such as cheese, blood and brains! It must have been well worth looking after a good strain.

"Good beer yeast lets itself be kept in two states, that dry and wet. If one wants to keep it in the wet state, so it must have fermented fast and be filled to the very brim in clean well stoppered and tarred bottles which are then kept in a cool cellar. Provided that there is no liquid present, neither water nor beer, the yeast will keep at least 3 weeks in summer and longer in winter. Should the yeast have become sour then wash it quickly with clean water, add sugar and some strong alcohol derived from grain, not fruit and a little wort and let this work for one hour before adding it to the main wort which is to be fermented.

Keeping the top yeast in a dry state is done thus:

One pours the wet yeast into a linen bag and lets all the liquid drain. Wash the yeast until it is quite clean and has but one colour. Dry the residue over tender heat until it is fully dried. Keep this in dry, well sealed containers until it is required and then take as much as you need and mix this with clean water.

Yeasts so prepared should be kept in a shady place buried one foot under the earth or sunk in a deep well".

I can't imagine an instance in which we would nowadays tar a container or bury it in the garden, but the general idea of preserving a yeast strain indefinitely can be generated from Hahn's description.

Failure to maintain a strain can be caused by lack of essential salts. One can either buy yeast nutrient or add a few grains of ammonium phosphate and potassium nitrate to the ferment.

Testing the Yeast.

The availability of packets of dried brewer's yeast has obviated to a large extent the need to test yeast samples for their viability. It is worth making a yeast starter when brewing on sultry summer days though, in order to get the wort fermenting quickly, for it is an empirical observation of many brewers and cooks, that things go off quicker in such weather. In order to minimise the risk of alien microbes invading and ruining the wort, the yeast is mixed with a little sugar and water an hour before it is needed and should be working well by the time it is added to the main body of the wort. The rapid saturation of the wort with carbon dioxide as well as the layer of yeast floating on the wort afford a very efficient protection.

The dried packet yeasts tend to produce a thin carpet of thick oily bubbles on the surface of the wort, whereas fresh samples of brewer's yeast yield a thick dense carpet of foam, rising in grotesque shapes, rather like a lunar landscape. The latter description is of course the way it should be.

If you try to establish your own strain you will be interested in some of the tips given by Hahn and his contemporaries to test its quality. Good yeast should be white in colour and when pressed, hold together rather as a dough. It should smell faintly of wine and have a pleasant sour taste. When shaken it should foam. If a few drops of wet yeast are poured into boiling water, they should denaturate rather as a poached egg-white does, and float on the surface. If it doesn't solidify, or sinks, then the yeast is of little value.

5. Theory of Malting.

Starch is Strength!

> *"Dank, Dank, Dank, sei dir, Osiris,*
> *Dank, Dank dir, Isis, gebracht!*
> *Es siegte die Stärke und krönet zum Lohn,*
> *die Schönheit und Weisheit mit ewiger Kron'."*

> *"Thanks, thanks, thanks be to you Osiris,*
> *Thanks be brought to you Isis.*
> *Strength triumphs and pays*
> *Beauty and wisdom with an eternal crown."*

(Die Zauberflöte. Final chorus)

Converting barley or any other cereal into malt uses a fundamental phase in the natural germination process in order to make a useful product. The maltster in ancient Egypt was probably the first to control such a biological process and thus produce a foodstuff on a large scale and was, according to legend a woman, for Herodotus in around 450 B.C. ascribed the art of brewing to Isis wife of Osiris, often referred to as Rameses II, who had lived about 1500 years earlier. I'm sure all beer lovers will be grateful to Mozart and his librettist Schikaneder for producing a grand finale in praise of the godly pair. Mozart's knowledge of their exact contribution to civilisation is not certain but the question is, were the puns on "Stärke", and "Kron", in the chorus intentional? German academics may crown me for suggesting it but it is inescapable that Schikaneder gave the supposed discoverer of beer lines containing "Stärke", which can mean "starch", or "strength", and "Krone", which may be a crown on the head or the head on beer. Such word plays are really too good to be coincidental and Mozart and Schikaneder were heavily into Free Masonry.

Hence the final chorus could be:

> *"Thanks be to you Osiris,*
> *Thanks be brought to you Isis,*
> *Starch rules and as payment crowns*
> *Beauty and wisdom with an eternal head."*

And in one of Sarastro's finest arias he sings,

> *"O Isis und Osiris schenket*
> *der Weisheit Geist dem neuen Paar!"*
> *"O Isis and Osiris give the spirit of Wisdom to the young couple."*

He believes the wisdom of Isis and Osiris to be a sound basis for a new marriage and one can hardly dispute its benefit in nuptial arrangements and not only for beer making! According to younger versions of the myth, after Osiris' murder and disembodiment, Isis found his penis and conceived her son Horus by it!

Most of a seed's volume is a starch store, or an energy reservoir to be called upon during germination. The start of germination is determined in nature by the temperature and soil dampness. If sufficient water is available then the seed takes up the water and can be seen to swell up over several hours.

Water is the universal transport medium in nature and once the seed has absorbed sufficient then the chemical reactions may commence whereby the starch is converted to sugar. The seed cannot use starch directly as an energy source so it calls up the enzymes diastase to break the starch down. Only in the presence of water can the enzymes move through the body of the seed, and get at the large molecules and convert them into useable units.

This is the same process which interests the brewer, for it is the sugar produced from the starch which he can ferment to make alcohol. The maltster uses the natural germinating process to produce enzymes which the brewer needs to convert the starch into sugar.

The maltster does this by creating the optimum conditions for the diastase to be produced and transported into the starchy body of the seed. At the same time, protein splitting enzymes are set to work on the large protein molecules, converting them into water soluble substances and thus providing clear, nutrient rich beer.

Having encouraged the production of the enzymes, the next process is their conservation so that they are ready for use when the brewer calls on them. This second part of the malting is achieved by drying the enzyme rich barley seeds at the right speed and temperature and it is this dried form of diastase and protease containing barley which we call malt. Provided the malt is correctly stored, it will last indefinitely, unlike barley which does go off.

To make malt, the following steps are carried out:

1)   Steeping the barley: the cistern.

Dry barley contains 12-14% water. The magnified unswollen corn has a wrinkled skin. In this state the seed keeps many years although it rapidly loses its germination powers. As long as insufficient water is present the seed germ is dormant for without water (the universal transport medium) the molecules can never meet, no sugar can be made and no vital energy food can be carried to the seed germ. As soon as water and warmth are supplied the seed begins to show signs of life.

The maltster prefers two rowed summer barley which, with its thick protecting husk, takes about two days at 10°C to take sufficient water on board. In fact the water content rises to about 45% and incredible forces are developed within the seed as the starch swells up. The osmotic pressure can be as high as 2000 atmospheres which is why the cistern holding our soaking barley must allow it to expand unhindered. Transporting barley in leaky hulled ships was a hazardous operation and many grain carriers were split asunder if their cargo became wet. In its swollen state the barley is bursting to start germinating.

The rate of water uptake can be accelerated by raising the temperature of the steep water but this would also increase the respiration of the seed and lead to valuable corn substance being lost as heat and carbon dioxide, as well as increasing the danger from mould spores. If temperatures too far below 10°C are used then the water uptake and respiration are too hindered and the corn "suffocates". This critical temperature explains why traditionally barley was malted and beer brewed between October and March.

The use of the term "respiration", sometimes sounds strange to the non-biologist but it is the oxidation of the carbon containing compounds such as sugar, by atmospheric oxygen, which supplies the energy for the germination and growth of plants and higher forms of life. Thus the barley must be able to take up adequate amounts of oxygen and discharge the carbon dioxide it produces.

Because of this the so-called "water/air" cistern has been in use for the last 100 years. By blowing air through the cistern, the steep water is replenished with oxygen and at the same time carbon dioxide swept out. One can steep the barley without this refinement but then the steep water must be regularly changed. This however slows down the growth of the germinating barley and as all our modern domestic water supplies contain chlorine, we would also be replenishing one of the germinating seed's biggest poisons.

Generally the length of the steep depends on the malt being made, but the limiting values are 48-100 hours, whereby 72 hours seems to be a good optimum. I have always found that the magic 45% water content is achieved in 3 days at temperatures between 8-10°C which just so happens to be the temperatures in the salad trays in your fridge. You may wish to start preparing your spouse now! I prefer to wait for winter and use the bicycle shed. It is always worth noting that Stopes in 1885 remarked, "I have not yet encountered three maltsters in Britain who take the trouble to ascertain the true temperature of the steep-liquor at any part of the process". We shall find time and again that good beer was brewed with scant regard to accurate temperature measurement but much bad beer was brewed too! I suspect that the good maltsters and brewers were the ones who got the temperature approximately right by instinct, not those who ignored it. The point is though that a few degrees either way is not going to make or break the brew.

The other vital point to successful malting is to keep all light out. If this is impossible then buy some blue paper and cover your cistern with it. Blue light will prevent photosynthesis and the production of chlorophyll, which alters the flavour of the beer for the worse.

2)   Germination.

"First, the husk or membrane which envelopes the component parts of the seed is swollen and bursts; the plumula, called by maltsters the acrospire, the part which produces the stem and the leaves, gradually expands, and when buried, rises to the surface of the soil; the radicle puts forth ramifications, and becomes a root. The cotyledon (or part of the seed which contains the matter for early nutrition of the young plant), which is originally insipid and farinaceous, becomes sweet and mucilaginous and furnishes materials for the early nutriment of the plant before its roots and leaves are adequate to their full functions."

(Ford. Treatise on Malting and Brewing. 1862.)

56

This flatulent description of germination provides us with vocabulary guaranteed to elicit immediate response in any pub off the Old Kent Road, but it also summarises beautifully the next and most important step in malting. Needless to say the germination is carried out in precise, controlled conditions in the modern malting and as we cannot and do not want to malt with industrial exactitude, we shall again reach back to historical sources for our methods.

There seem to have been two common procedures for securing good germination. One was to spread the swollen barley on wire trays to a depth of about 30-40 cm. These heaps were turned twice daily with wooden forks in order to distribute any dampness, and allow trapped carbon dioxide and heat to escape. The other method was to "couch", the barley in the cistern by simply allowing the steep-liquor to run off and letting the grain start to germinate in situ. Because of the relatively small quantities of malt which we shall make, we shall in fact have to use a combination of both methods. To make a heap 40cm deep requires more barley than we can successfully handle in one go, and to use shallower heaps results in this so called, 'young heap,' drying too quickly. On the other hand, our cistern will probably be a bucket and if we couch in the bucket we shall have a couched heap of 50 cm depth, which is about right.

The advantages of couching the wet barley in the bucket in which it was steeped are that with a little imagination we can convert our bucket into a pneumatic malter which is far less dependent on external temperature and speeds up germination.

A bucket can also be cloistered in any cupboard of about the right temperature far easier than a somewhat amorphous heap of wet barley on a tray. Furthermore the pneumatic malter will require your attention at the most once a day and then for a far shorter period of time than a wet heap. Because fresh, damp air of the correct temperature is constantly being forced up through the couch there is no fear of the germination being disturbed by drying out or suffocation. These considerations far outweigh the main advantage of a tray, which is that you can see easier what is going on within the barley and is perhaps less work initially to set up but more on couch construction later.

The temperature within the couch should not exceed 20°C nor drop below 10°C. Ideally it should be between 12-15°C and in winter this temperature can be easily maintained. A shady airy building or shed in summer should allow you to keep below 20°C excepting during the rare hot spells we occasionally get. The green malt will however give off heat and the centre of the heap can become very hot in summer, reaching temperatures in excess of 50°C. This can only be avoided by turning the malt frequently. Sprinkling the heap with water cannot be recommended.

Morphological changes during germination.

Even if the wet heap in the couch appears to be drying out, it probably isn't. The seed in fact will continue to absorb any residual moisture available to it and so the grain surface becomes drier whilst the corn inner is becoming wetter. By weighing the couch and contents before germination commences you can check to see if any weight loss which could be associated with drying out, occurs. Despite appearances, there will be no change in mass.

After about 12-14 hours in the couch or on the tray, the first signs of life become apparent in the form of tiny white tips which are the precursors of the root system. If you have steeped using an air/water cistern, these "eyes" may be already visible before the steeping process is complete, showing how much time may be saved by aeration.

In the following days the primary and secondary root systems will reveal themselves and within 2-3 days of the steep being finished, four or so root strands should be clearly visible. The seeds may start to sweat and now is the time when possible suffocation can occur so the heap should be turned every 6-8 hours unless a pneumatic couch is used. According to the literature the smell of the couch should be that of fresh apples although I find cucumber a more apt description. It should certainly be easy on the nose!

During this time the acrospire which is to become the first leaf, has been developing under the husk and it only reveals itself as a slight swelling on one side of the seed. If the husk is carefully peeled back, the acrospire is clearly visible. This "green malt", as it is called, should be ready for drying after about 5-6 days on a tray, when the acrospire is ⅔ the length of the seed. This is a critical point to observe for if the acrospire is allowed to continue to grow beyond this length, valuable corn substance is lost, to the detriment of the final beer. If allowed to, the roots will form a felted impenetrable mass, which is surprisingly difficult to pull apart. Further growth of the acrospire must be prevented and as this is done by drying the green malt in an even and careful way, we cannot proceed with a sodden felted lump of untended germinated barley. Whenever turning the heap, the maltster takes great care to break up the felt before it becomes a major and laborious chore. This task may not be neglected.

If a pneumatic malter has been used, then the heap should only be turned about once per day, provided the temperature does not rise above tolerable limits. The acrospire should be the right length after about 5 days but a check should be made every day. Germination on trays may take up to 5 days longer.

3) The carbon dioxide bath.

During the last century continental maltsters developed a rather elegant method of improving their malt. As stated, the object of malting is to produce enzymes which can break down the starch and protein molecules into units which the growing plant can use as energy for its development. To do this, the maltster has to allow the seed to grow, thus using up valuable corn substance. Traditionally the green malt is dried to prevent further use of the available starch and protein, but this leaves many large molecules in an unusable state. The mashing process will break down the starch molecules but does not impress the heavy albumin and gluten molecules. If however the seed is left wet and alive, but the necessary oxygen is withheld, the enzymes continue to work on the large protein and starch molecules, rendering them water soluble for inclusion in the beer, but use of the starch in the form of sugar by the maturing acrospire is prevented. The easiest way to accomplish this is to allow the acrospire to achieve the magic ⅔ of the corn length, turn off the air pump and allow the carbon dioxide to accumulate in the bucket. It is important not to kill the seed off with this treatment, but the green malt survives three days at 15°C with no air. Don't forget that the green malt must still be turned once daily. If the acrospire is obviously still increasing in length, then too much air is present and the treatment should be ceased. Provided this is not the case, the result is a much more soluble and workable malt.

Summary

Germination takes 7-10 days. The first phase consists of steeping the barley in cold water to allow it to take up the necessary moisture to grow. If the steep is aerated, the green malt is ready in 5-6 days. After steeping, excess water is drained off and the barley allowed to commence growing so that it produces the required enzymes. It continues growing in an oxygen deficient atmosphere until the acrospire is about ⅔ the length of the seed.

Darker malts require less accurate attention and may be left to germinate longer and warmer and need turning less often. Lighter malts must never have an acrospire of longer than ¾ the corn length and if this length cannot be adhered to through some unforeseen circumstance, then the green malt is kilned more intensely and thus converted to a into a darker variety as described in the malt recipes later. The charts in chapter 8 show the allowable distribution of acrospire length for different types of malt.

If germination is sufficiently far advanced to consider drying the green malt, the starchy white centre of the corn should feel dry and may be rubbed between the fingers, (farinaceous as Ford calls it). If the corn substance feels slimy, then the germination was probably carried out too quickly.

Drying the green malt.

The process of drying the malt is to prevent further unproductive consumption of the corn substance by the acrospire. Without water the enzymes cannot be transported through the starchy body of the seed to break down the starch into sugar, nor can the sugars be transported to the cotyledon for use by the developing acrospire. The drying process however must not destroy the sensitive enzymes and hence so long as the green malt is wet, drying temperatures below 40°C are essential. Once most of the water has been removed, the enzymes are less labile and can withstand temperatures of 60-100°C. In fact this drying process for pale malts is more like a withering and in the sorts of ovens at our disposal, will take 2 days. You will be extremely fortunate to have a baking oven which will maintain temperatures of 30-40°C and even if you have, it is most unlikely that it may be commandeered for several days at a time. Airing cupboards and fan heaters come into their own here but don't forget to keep out the light.

Normally the damp green malt is loaded onto specially constructed wire trays and dried in a stream of warm air. Sometimes the malt would first be withered by spreading it thinly on a large floor and left to dry, with occasional turning, at less than 30°C. This may have been done to save coal or wood. The chances of the malt going off or becoming mouldy during this withering, is quite high, but Hahn records that in order to save the cost of a kiln and firing it, it was common to make excellent malt using this slow form of drying. Air dried malts of this type, make a slightly sour beer, but Hahn claims that they are in no way inferior to kilned malts.

If the intention is to make a pale malt, then drying will reduce the water content to about 2-4%. Careful weighing of the green malt and trays is necessary before the drying may proceed for the water content must be accurately determined so that one can carefully follow the progress of the malting. These mass changes and their importance are amplified in appendix 3. The dried malt must also be friable and produce a chalky trace when rubbed on an abrasive surface. Should a darker malt be required, then far less attention need be paid to the temperature of this drying process. The higher roasting temperatures of dark malts destroy the enzymes anyway and the glassy quality of a fast dried malt is actually desirable.

During the drying stage, the temperature of the wet green malt is always below the air temperature in the drying cabinet. This is because the evaporating water takes heat from the malt in order to change from water to water vapour. One observes the same effect when standing in a draught after the bath. As the malt dries, its temperature converges with the air temperature. When these are equal, the malt is dry enough to kiln. One should however gain supporting evidence by weighing the malt and calculating its percentage water. Once the water content is approaching zero, the malt may be kilned. The temperature for this process varies from between 45-145°C depending on the exact nature, pale, amber, dark, crystal or black, of the malt to be made. Exact graphs of mass changes and suitable temperatures for drying and kilning a variety of malts, are given in chapter 8 on malt recipes.

Storing the malt.

Before the roasted malt is stored, it is advisable to remove the dried roots from the corn. This is a laborious task and I have often omitted it although most literature insists that the roots have a negative effect on the beer quality. As can be seen from Dreverhoff's figures in appendix 3, the malt is hydroscopic and takes up water slowly. If we wait until the malt is to be used, then the roots are no longer so brittle and removing them is an even bigger chore. The malster has mechanical means of tumbling the malt in a drum, using the collisions of the grains with each other to break off the roots. I have done it by rubbing the grains by hand, but a tin can with some clean stones, half filled with malt and shaken, works well.

The malt may be stored in air-tight polythene bags, which will prevent the uptake of too much water. Dreverhoff allowed his malt to increase to 2% water, which is not only acceptable but according to some maltsters, necessary. Malt allowed to take up more than 5% becomes "slack" and cannot be used in that wet state. Before polythene, slack malt was an ever present problem, normally solved by re-roasting to produce a dark malt, which could then be used as an adjunct to the main body of pale malt.

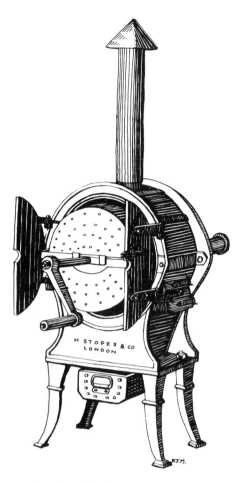

H STOPES & CO
LONDON

F.J.M.

Stopes patented a delightful construction for the purpose of roasting slack malt and converting it into a darker type, thus avoiding wasting it entirely. He records that in the 19th century, no brewer in England or on the Continent was without such a malt roaster as they constantly had to convert slack pale malt into dark malt. This indicates that the "popularity" of dark beers at that time had perhaps more to do with necessity than taste. Dark malts contain no enzymes and the introduction of the saccharometer in the early 19th century revealed that these malts produce little extract for the brewer, providing some taste but mainly colouring. Hence they are something of a luxury in brewing economics which explains the hard sell light beers receive these days. Dark beers were probably brewed to cover some shortcoming or other in the malting or brewing process.

Malt should be left 4 weeks to mature, and if it is to be allowed to take up its 2% water, a well shutting cardboard box is best employed. As soon as the water content has risen to 2% transfer the malt to sealed plastic bags. Appendix 3 has a comprehensive set of mass changes during malting, based on 2.5 kg. barley starting weight. This should assist those afraid of the sums.

Quality of malt.

Many eminent maltsters describe the qualities to look for in a good malt. The only easy test, apart from studying the overall mass gains during malting, is to measure the percentage germination of the barley. The professional maltster achieves a 99% germination rate, which I have as yet never done. 90% seems a good average, but then I never know exactly how old the barley is that I buy in. The percentage of glassy grains, as against powdery ones, is also a useful guide. Not above 5% should be glassy but if the germination rate is lower, then so the percentage of glassy grains will be higher.

A novel method of the 18th and 19th centuries was to float the malt. I suspect that brewers then, as now, were incorrigible children at heart and thus enjoyed playing submarines. Hahn wrote, "In order to see if the finished malt is well kilned and made accordingly from good barley, one takes a dish with water, throws in some such handfuls of malt and stirs it around. The insufficiently malted grains sink to the bottom, the half-malted float only with one end and in a vertical position, the attended and well malted grains will swim."

The very best indication of successful malting remains though, the mass changes during the various stages. Provided we keep the percentage of germinated, friable grains above 85% we shan't go far wrong, for the difference between 85% and 95% good grains lies not so much in the quality of the resulting beer, but in the economics of large scale brewing.

Grinding the malt.

Malts, especially dark malts, are extremely hard. In order to extract the sugar and protein, the brewer has to break the husk of the malt and render the interior corn substance open to the hot water, with which it will be washed out. Thus the malt has to be crushed. The particle size of the ground malt is however critical. If the malt is reduced to the consistency of flour, the water can gain excellent access to the corn substance, but does not drain out. The problem is that the particles of flour must be larger than the sieve through which they are being drained, or the sieve will block. If the particles are too big, then access of the water to the sugar is hindered, and the sugar remains in the corn substance instead of dissolving up in the water. In practice the corns of malt should be broken into 2 or 3 pieces. This allows not only optimum access of the water but also good draining of the spent husks without blocking the sieve.

The problem is that kitchen machines and coffee grinders all reduce the malt to flour. Rolling pins and other such implements have little effect on the malt and so most home brewers end up using a coffee grinder and then cursing their blocked sieves. Juch (1842) admonishes his readers to always dampen their malt before it is taken to the mill. This he did by spreading the malt on boards and spraying it with water from a watering can. The malt was then left in summer for 8-12, in winter for 12-16 hours and then taken to the mill. The malt had to have just the right dampness. Too wet and it was squashed to a pulp and became warm, too dry and it was reduced to flour. This method is worth a try in conjunction with the kitchen machine. You must use the malt so prepared immediately for mashing but even then it is inevitable that such treatment alters the beer, but that is where the fun lies. It is a matter of personal taste as to whether this is acceptable. I find that my historical recipe beers produce grimaces the first time from my friends but they never actually stop drinking and always come back for more. We are used to standard beers and so our palates sometimes need re-educating.

Many kitchen machines now have wheat grinding attachments which should be ideal for breaking the malt provided they can be set to grind very coarsely. One can also fit a standard 4 inch carborundum wheel to a variable speed power drill in a drill stand and work wonders with an old saucepan as the stationary surface.

Crushed malt which is too farinaceous has always been a problem and hence historical brewing literature reveals the solution. Use a mash bucket fitted with a tap and a false wire bottom, as described in the German recipes. This encourages the spent husks to form a coarse bed which the floury corn substance won't block, but more on this later.

6. Theory of Mashing.

"The old Bavarian brewer is no chemist, and it wouldn't be right if he were one. But his practices are so chemically correct that he always produces with exactitude that which is needed; a good, clear, healthy, well keeping drink."

(Anon)

The unknown German writer of about 100 years ago again highlights the most important thing to remember: you can get it right without deep scientific understanding. If the last chapter scared you, skip this one and go straight to the recipes. Enjoy a couple of brews and then come back for the theory.

I hope after the last chapter some malt is on, or there may even be some ready for brewing. If it has been well made and kept, it should be hard but powdery, (if that seems a contradiction, think of a stick of chalk) but under no circumstances of a glassy quality unless it is only a dark malt for colouring. The grains smell pleasantly sweet of that typical malty flavour. This sweetness does not indicate a high concentration of sugar. In fact malt contains only about 10% maltose and its sweet taste is more an indication of the speed with which the amylase can convert starch into sugar as soon as the necessary warmth and dampness is supplied by the tongue. This apart, the diastase in our saliva will also supplement the activity of the enzymes in the malt. The mashing process will use the same enzymatic activity to break down the remaining starch (55% of the total corn substance) into fermentable sugar. The old Bavarian brewer learnt by experience how to get it right, but here is the chemical explanation of what he did in order to achieve an optimum yield and steer his process to render a good beer.

Alpha and Beta Amylase and the Dextrines.

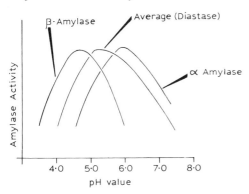

During the mashing of the malt, the alpha amylase enzyme splits the long starch chains, consisting of thousands of glucose units, into shorter dextrine molecules, (approximately ten glucose units). Alpha amylase requires about 65°C, an aqueous medium and a pH of about 5.7 in order to work at its best. The temperature is important because the conversion must be brought about as speedily as possible in order to reduce the risk of infection from alien microbes. Without water the movement of the enzymes and starch is zero and so the necessary collisions required to bring about the breaking up of the starch cannot occur. The pH seems to be the one at which destruction of the complicated enzyme molecules by the high temperature is slowest for 65°C is much higher than any natural biological process uses and so the enzymes do have it rather hotter than nature intended. The alpha amylase are tough types and will handle temperatures up to 80°C so there is no reason to excessively worry about any local hot spots in your mash tub.

The dextrines are still too big for yeast to ferment easily and certainly too large for the acrospire to handle and so the corn calls up the second row in its enzyme arsenal, the

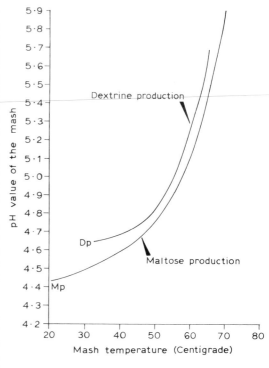

beta amylase. The beta amylase are happiest at 55°C and a pH value of about 4.7. They are thermally more labile than the alpha and don't want to spend too long above 70°C or they will be irreversibly destroyed. This apparent contradiction which the two enzymes present us with, their likes and dislikes, is actually of use to the brewer. If he mashes hot, he destroys some of the beta amylase and ends up with a dextrine rich beer for the yeast ferments the dextrines only with difficulty. This means less alcohol but high nourishment even after the necessary prolonged maturing process. A low mash temperature gives a thinner beer of higher alcohol content and faster clearing properties. As a general rule of thumb, a pH value of between 5.1-5.3 and a temperature of about 65°C should give a maltose to dextrine ratio of about 3:1. A lager beer though needs the slow fermentation of the dextrines to produce the qualities peculiar to it. This slow fermentation process occurs during the maturation of the young beer and thus lager beers, most dark beers, which are brewed for flavour not alcohol, and the strong beers which should contain nourishment as well as alcohol, are all mashed at over 68°C. This favours the alpha amylase and slowly destroys the beta. The weaker beers (no value judgement intended) are mashed at about 62-64°C which means that if you want a beer ready for the middle of next week, mash at a low temperature.

The mash, pH and enzymes.

This beautifully refined process of mashing has yet one more elegant surprise, guaranteed to make us believe the world is the brewer's oyster. It is convenient to start the mash with an amount of water which produces a porridge consistency in the mash tun. This allows the brewer to maintain his temperature for the operation of the alpha amylase by adding hot or boiling water to the tun during the mash. These are in fact just the conditions which favour the conservation of the enzymes, for they are not encouraged to leave the protective environment of the corn substance with its ideal pH. Starch is not very water soluble so this in no way inhibits the enzyme operation. As the mash cools, it is diluted by the home-brewer who adds hot water to maintain a reasonable temperature. This more dilute environment suits the beta amylase which along with the water soluble dextrines leave the corn. The existence of the already produced maltose has now itself a protecting effect on the enzymes and so they are better able to withstand the hostile world outside the corn substance.

The porridge mash does have its disadvantages. It is more difficult to stir and as convection within the thick slurry is non-existent, it is difficult to prevent and eliminate local hot spots within the mash. Furthermore, keeping the reaction product (maltose) in high concentration, does slow down the reaction, and so lengthen the mash time. The effectiveness of the alpha and beta amylase is considerably reduced by the incorrect pH. The problem seems to be that at pH 7, a temperature of 65°C destroys them twice as fast as at pH 5. Most tap water, especially in an area with temporary hard water, has a pH above 7 and may need softening. If the correct malt types have been chosen for a particular water type, the pH should be at the optimum value without any adjustment by the brewer.

Iodine test for starch conversion.

In the presence of iodine solution, the starch forms a strong blue coloured compound, in which the iodine positions itself in the spiral chains of the starch. If the starch has all been converted to dextrine, then this reaction cannot take place, and one knows that the time is right to allow the beta amylase to take over. The mash, which now has a dextrine to maltose ratio of about 3:2, is diluted and allowed to cool a little. This dextrine conversion end point will take at least 30 minutes at 65°C to occur and at 63°C as long as an hour.

At 63°C the beta amylase will have been well protected, and can now have the next 90 minutes to break some of the dextrines down into maltose. The longer one allows the malt to mash, the greater the final conversion to maltose will be, but the normally hoped for 3:1 maltose:dextrine ratio should be achieved within two hours. Mash times of more than eight hours have little to recommend them.

One sees that the home-brewer stands no chance of making a standardised beer, for he will never make exactly the same beer twice. Assuming he had the patience to try and control the parameters, his thermometer, kitchen balance and clock are not accurate enough to allow the necessary delicate control. No wonder the old Bavarian brewer was not interested in chemistry!

Heating up or cooling down?

There are two ways of arriving at the right temperature for the mash. The simplest and least dangerous for the enzymes is of course to start with a cold mash and slowly warm it to 65°C. One would have to be quite negligent before a too higher mash temperature were reached. Most English recipes however do exactly the opposite. The malt is infused with water hot enough it is judged, to give the right temperature when mixed with the cold malt. Thus a "strike" temperature as it is called, of 72°C should give a thick mash of 63°C. Hot spots are avoided by vigorous stirring, but not with the thermometer. Thermometers aren't in fact particularly delicate but they do have their limits and if one does break there is no option but to throw away the mash and start again. The mercury is most dangerous if ingested or inhaled. There is little point in taking any temperature measurements unless the mash has been well stirred. A temperature gradient of 10°C between the top and centre of the mash is quite possible. These hot spots can be evened out by thorough mixing and the addition of hot or cold water.

This English method is commonly referred to as the "infusion" mash and has the obvious advantage for the home brewer in that it is relatively simple to operate. On the continent though the decoction method is almost exclusively used. There are many variations and a number of these are given in the chapter on recipes, but the general idea is as follows.

The crushed malt is mixed with water at about 35°C. After a few hours ⅓ of the mash is removed and heated firstly to 70°C then after a short pause, brought to the boil. The boiling mash is then added to the main body of malt which after stirring should be at around 50-55°C. This process is repeated and the temperature brought up to 65°C and after the third run and about 5 hours, a final mash temperature of over 75°C is reached. Some light beers are made using only a two mash process (Zweimaischverfahren) for the important 60-65°C maltose conversion temperature is reached after the second mash boil. There is also a highly effective high temperature, short mash process (Hochkurzmaischverfahren). The malt is initially mashed in at 62°C in a similar way to the English infusion method, but after 20 minutes a small quantity is removed and boiled so that when recombined with the main mash, the temperature rises to 68-72°C. This then wrecks the beta amylase and provides for a dextrine rich beer.

Using temperatures so far above the optimum for the enzymes does of course destroy them but as the brewer is not only interested in the production of maltose and dextrines, the continental method does contain its logic. The decoction method increases the time allowed for the breaking down of complicated protein molecules which in their smaller water soluble form are dissolved in the beer. This is extremely important when using gluten rich barley types as these heavy sticky molecules require different temperatures and enzymes in order to be broken down. Some German recipes include the so called "protein break", whereby the mash is held at the optimum temperature for protein conversion into smaller molecules by the protease enzymes. English patriots claim that the higher quality UK barley types don't require this decoction treatment, whilst German brewers think that English beer is not worth drinking because it has only been infused. Fortunately the home brewer doesn't need to be hide bound by such prejudice. The point is that cloudy beers result from not enough attention being paid to the needs of the protease enzymes and the fact that at the strike temperatures of the infusion process they are completely destroyed. This leaves the nitrogen containing albumen and globulin in their heavy insoluble state to form a suspension in the beer. An hour or two at forty degrees however leaves the enzymes time enough to go to work on these molecules.

Decocting is a skilled and somewhat hazardous process in the domestic kitchen and much more labour intensive. It is best to use infusion recipes unless one has the time and no one else, especially children, under one's feet. A cloudy beer is not such a catastrophe provided the taste is right and there can be little doubt that today's crystal clear product has more to do with the radical filtration process used than the skill of any brewer.

The problem of protein cloudiness was solved in the UK prior to filtration, by using starch sources which contained less protein, to stretch the expensive malt. Thus maize and rice have been in use for many years, especially when the harvest was poor. These so called grits were often cheaper to purchase and free of malt tax, which didn't mean that the consumer wasn't invited to pay the full tax as if the beer had only been made from malt! As indicated earlier, the German *Reinheitsgebot*, forbids the use of any starch source other than malted barley and thus Germans are horrified to find that the English brewer wants to sell a product in Germany which doesn't have the right to be called "Bier". The English were not too happy to be told that their best bitter wasn't up to scratch either! The one thing they all want to do though is earn money and here the poor protein has a charge to answer too. Protein haze wasn't much of a problem until the turn of the century when the use of mineral fertilizers became wide-spread. Harvests reached new records and the brewer was a happy man because malt prices sank which improved his profits. Then, because of the change in agricultural methods, the protein haze started to be a problem, presumably because protein richer barley types were in use, and consumer resistance was felt. Suddenly the English brewer, who had always been envied his much simpler infusion process, was the one with a cloudy outlook. He could have scrapped the new breweries, which were the product of the technological leap forward of the industrial revolution, and gone over to the continental method, or even tried to go back to the old fashioned agricultural methods which had served so well, so long, but the increased use of grits seemed a far simpler (and more profitable) solution.

The Reinheitsgebot, which forbade any such simple solutions, made the German brewer much more inventive. Suppose he wanted to use the "Hot quick-mash method", (*Hochkurzmaischverfahren*) in order to save time and fuel costs, he had the problem of no protein break in the mash process. What he did was to allow the wort after mashing and washing, to cool to 40°C and to add to this a fresh aliquot of malt which had been taken from a 40°C mash. This was then maintained at this temperature for about 30 minutes, heated once more to 70°C, strained and boiled with the hops. One sees that from a historical standpoint, expediency has always ruled over technique. The house-brewer

A Beer Machine by Hahn (without wheels).

should allow himself the same latitude. I shall return to proteins and hop boiling later.

Having touched on the dangers of decocting in the modern domestic kitchen, it is worth considering a novel "Beer Machine", invented by that inspiration to house-brewers, Johann Gottfried Hahn. A re-creation of how things looked in Hahn's kitchen when he was brewing is worthwhile. The tun in which he mashed has a false bottom about ⅔ the way up. This false bottom was perforated with fairly large holes and covered with a straw mat or linen cloth. The crushed malt was placed on the mat or cloth and the brewing water in the lower part of the tun heated by means of a fire under the tun, until it was just too hot for the brewer to dip his hand in which would probably be around 65°C. Then water was ladled out of the bottom of the tun by opening a small trap-door in the false bottom. The door then was closed and the hot water poured over the malt through which it drained, mashing the malt as it did so. This process was continued until the malt-sugar had been thoroughly extracted.

The temperature of the wort was presumably allowed to rise during mashing because at some point the hops were added to the wort in the lower vessel and the beer flavoured at the same time as mashing progressed. Hahn was particularly proud of his beer machine because he claimed it could be taken to the field of combat by soldiers (on wheels perhaps) and they could brew between manoeuvres. He doesn't tell if the army took up his idea.

Washing the draff.

After mashing, the wort has to be separated from the spent malt grains, called draff. The wort contains all the water soluble extract from the malt, which the beer is to be fermented from. It should need no emphasis that it is the most costly fruit of our labours thus far. The problem is that the malt grains do not yield up the wort easily. When it has been wrested from the grains, being a sweet sugary solution, it is a perfect nutrient for the Armadas of microbes lurking, ready to rape and pillage. The latter problem is not too acute, for the wort has still to be boiled for at least an hour, which will thoroughly sterilise it. The draff is an excellent animal food and if added to the dough when baking bread provides much needed extra roughage, but the problems of relieving it of the last vestiges of wort are the most intractable in the whole brewing process. I weep at the amount of good wort which I've fed to my neighbours' rabbits for want of an adequate extraction method.

If the malt was ground to a fine powder before mashing, you will now reap the reward of your sin and error. The draff will pack itself to a solid mass and hours of work will not produce a satisfactory extraction of the wort. The wash water will not penetrate the draff and hangs in the surface few centimetres of the draff, only to eventually run away through a few channels it has made for itself. In a desperate attempt to rescue the trapped wort, the home-brewer uses gallons of wash water which only leads to new problems, for the fine flour will immediately block any sieve or filter available. The brewer stands there like the Sorcerer's Apprentice with the volume of water increasing and the rate of wash-water flow decreasing.

Should the malt be ground too coarsely then the mash water will not penetrate the corn substance and enzyme activity won't develop. The starch which has been incompletely converted to sugar is then difficult to wash out of the draff, again for want of water penetration.

Provided the malt has been broken rather than crushed, these problems shouldn't arise. The rough husks, which have a tendency to settle out more quickly than any floury particles, form an excellent filter bed which entrains the fine particles, and provided there aren't too many of them, won't block. This allows the use of an exceedingly coarse sieve or colander to hold the draff.

Most home-brew books recommend washing the draff by fixing a cloth stretched across a tun, placing the draff on the cloth and spraying the draff with hot water from a watering can. Don't believe it! This method of extracting the wort is called sparging, sounds fine and is approximately the domestic equivalent of the large brewery sparge, but that it doesn't work. With the amount of malt we use, it is impossible to sparge slowly enough with a watering can without either flooding the draff, which causes the water to run away in channels without percolating the mass of grains, or allowing the sparge water to get cold, which reduces the effectiveness of the extraction and doesn't provide for an extra session of enzyme activity: a sort of a "post mash". Thus I use the method common in the UK and on the Continent in the last century, and actually mash a second time with a second aliquot of nearly boiling water. This *Nachmaischen* as the German brewer calls it, ensures complete penetration of all the corn material by very hot water, which can be strained off, or even better, run out of a tap at the bottom of the mash tun. If the mash is well stirred before the wort is run off, then the fine powdery particles, which settle out more slowly than the large malt lumps, are at the top of the draff and cannot block the sieve. The large malt particles form their own sieve and one can then sparge in the same bucket as one mashed in. The sparge water can be gently run out of a kettle onto the surface of the draff, which is easier than struggling with a watering can or shower head. After this second mash, which only need last 15-20 minutes, the draff is strained through a coarse colander, (assuming you haven't used a mash tun with a tap, as described above) and then in the same vessel, washed with a slow trickle of boiling water from a wall boiler or kettle.

The draff is now pressed in order to squeeze the last dregs of liquid from it. If these pressed out drops do not taste of sugar, then the sparging may be considered finished. A few grains of the draff should also be chewed to make sure they are not sweet. The husks should be virtually empty of any corn substance.

At the end of the sparging there should be about 15-25 l. of wort and washings from 2.5 kg of malt. This volume has still to be boiled and may not be exceeded without good reason. In practice this is about as much as one can safely handle. It must be born in mind that the hot pot of hopped wort may still have to be moved from a warm kitchen to somewhere cool. This need to keep the volume small is the reason why the sparging must be as effective as possible.

If we were only to wash the draff by stirring it several times with batches of hot water, we would need more water than the above described sparge method demands. If you've ever rinsed soap from the washing by hand, you'll know that rinsing several times with a small amount of water is more effective than using the same total volume of water in a few large rinses. The sparging process attempts to optimize the rinsing by supplying many small, fresh portions of water.

Müller, however, was satisfied with two mashes and just straining the draff. He describes sometimes mashing a third time with cold water, running the third mash into the boiling hopped wort, and then running the hot wort back through the draff (see recipe for Koventbier). However, he does not seem to have been blessed with a hydrometer, and thus could remain blissfully unaware of the exact effectiveness of his mashing and sparging. The hydrometer allows us to measure the density of the wort and provided we know the volume of water used, we can calculate the amount of extract our mashing process has produced (see appendix 5). Hahn with his brewing machine definitely had the simplest method but it did have the disadvantage of not allowing him to ever leave his mash unattended. All other methods leave plenty of time for baking bread, making wine or tending the goats.

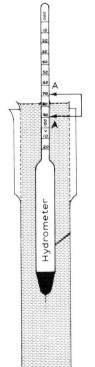

Measuring Relative Density.

Archimedes found that any body sinks so far into a liquid, until it has displaced its own mass of that liquid. Then it begins to float. It follows from this, that the volume of displaced liquid becomes smaller the denser the liquid is: i.e. the denser the liquid, the better things float in that liquid. The hydrometer uses this principle to measure the density of liquids. It is essentially a glass tube whose bottom end is loaded with lead shot. The top end of the tube is calibrated with a scale from which the relative density can be directly read by noting how far the hydrometer sinks into the liquid being tested. The water level (not the top of the meniscus) is taken as the mark against which the relative density is read off the hydrometer.

In pure water the hydrometer sinks to the 1.000 mark and in a 25% sugar solution to 1.090. This then is the range our hydrometer should cover for brewing purposes and provided you buy a hydrometer from a home-brew shop, you will be given one with this scale. Home-brew hydrometers will also have two other scales, one of which allows the amount of extract in the wort to be read in terms of how many pounds of sugar this wort is equivalent to, and the other, which is by far the most useful, reads off what alcohol concentration, as a percentage, will be produced in the beer after full fermentation of the available sugar.

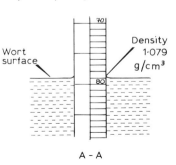

Wort surface

Density 1·079 g/cm³

A - A

Temperature and Relative Density.

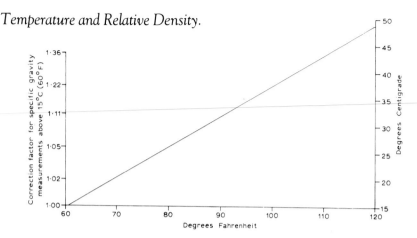

Correction factor for specific gravity measurements above 15°C (60°F) vs Degrees Fahrenheit / Degrees Centigrade

The advantages of using a hydrometer are enormous and being cheap, no home-brewer should be without one. The hydrometer is only accurate at the temperature at which it was calibrated. The volume of a liquid alters through expansion or contraction due to temperature changes and so the quotient *density = mass/volume* changes too. This is something of a nuisance as our wort is rarely at exactly the right temperature for density measurements and adjusting the temperature without adding water, is a troublesome affair. Nowadays most hydrometers are calibrated for room temperature which is generally accepted as being 20°C. If you get into studying old brewing literature in a quest for interesting recipes, then it is worth noting that normal room temperature was considered to be much lower in the eighteenth century and Twaddle hydrometers are calibrated at 15°C. It is also important to know that until quite recently density was measured in all sorts of peculiar units, the magnitude and manifold variety of which is outside the scope of this book. If you need any conversion tables, then a good general knowledge encyclopedia in the local library is invaluable.

Provided that your hydrometer is calibrated for use at 20°C then the graph allows you to read off a correction factor by which the measured density must be multiplied in order to achieve a true value.

Calculating the final alcohol concentration.

The importance of the hydrometer to the brewer can be best judged by considering the strange lengths the authorities went to in order to check the initial gravity of a brew. The most colourful, and thus most quoted went thus:

The appointed beer tester appeared at a pre-arranged time at the brewery (public house) and the brewmaster poured an accepted aliquot of beer over a wooden bench. The tester sat in the beer, and in Germany usually wore stag's leather trousers for this purpose. He remained thus seated for a recognised time, his mood being maintained by more conventional testing of a doubtless representative sample of the beers, and then he attempted to stand up. Dried beer is

72

very sticky and the tester assessed the original gravity of the beer by the difficulty he had in releasing himself from the wood bank. A beer of the very highest gravity had to lift the bank under the tester's backside. Although this method of testing is completely commensurate with the philosophy of house-brewing, the hydrometer is cheaper, less messy and in the long run far more accurate.

The hydrometer is dipped into a sample of the wort and sparge water and the relative density or end alcohol concentration read off. If the value is 1.045 then running the eye round the stem of the hydrometer to the appropriate scale allows one to read off the final alcohol concentration of 6.5%.

Suppose 15 l. of wort and washings would provide an alcohol concentration of 6.5%. If this was to be reduced to 4.5%, which would be an average Pils, then water is added until a relative density of 1.030 is reached. Approximately how much water to add can be calculated and examples are given in appendix 4, wherein light is also cast on the riddle of relative density.

The addition of sugar.

As already stated, the addition of sugar is treated with the utmost contempt in some countries. In fact though the use of household sugar need not be to the disadvantage of the beer and does stretch the wort a little. The question is always one of amount! Provided the sugar is not more than 20% of the total extract, I doubt that the most conscientious German Braumeister could tell that the beer has had sugar added. If for example, 1 kg of sugar was added to wort of density $1.045 g/cm^3$ extracted purely from the malt, this would be about 34% of the total extract being supplied by household sugar and freely must be the upper limit of what is acceptable. The product would certainly be drinkable but wouldn't taste much like a 4.5% Pils brewed only from malt. The problem is that the sugar only raises the alcohol content, not the nutrients such as proteins and dextrines. Hence the beer begins to taste too thin for its high alcohol content which leads to over-consumption and hangovers!

For those of us who like to know how well we have mashed, a further set of calculations can produce a percentage effectiveness. Appendix 5 contains such a sample calculation as well as an analysis of mash effectiveness achieved by some brewers from the Austrian Tyrol some 100 and 250 years ago.

7. Finishing the work.

The joy of the finished work:- "what sort of idea will they be able to make; those who have never seen it?"

Diary of Rupert II. von Ottobeuren from 15th January 1729 upon the completion of repairs to Kloster Ottobeuren.

Finishing a monastery meant that Rupert could then finally get at his beers. Throughout history, the lay brothers, along with ale wives, were the great brewers. The plan of the ideal monastery of St. Gallen was never realised but it was conceived with a wine and beer cellar and bakery/brewery for the monks, another brewery for important guests and another bakery/brewery for pilgrims. All this required a silo, mill, maltings, and cooper's shop as well as a garden for the herbs. It is difficult to comprehend on what a large scale ecclesiastical breweries operated. Monckton calculates that the 9th century, 18 foot steeping vessel of Fountains Abbey gave the monastery a capacity of around 900 barrels of ale per year, (260,000 pints). Kept in perspective though, neighbouring Rievaulx Abbey boasted at its height in the 12th century, 140 monks and 500 lay brothers and assuming the capacity of Fountains, that provided a mere one pint per day per brother! It must have been a colossal task to hew sufficient firewood, then boil and spice the wort, but they always took the trouble for boiling the wort fulfils five separate tasks.

1) The strongest taste component in beer is provided by the hops. This aroma only percolates into the wort when the hops are boiled in the wort for at least one hour. The hop flowers don't themselves contain the chemicals which provide the taste in the beer. During the boiling, the taste components are formed by isomerisation of the hop chemicals. Without boiling, the aroma producers aren't formed. This will variously be the case for herb beers too.

2) In order to preserve the delicate ratio of maltose to dextrines which our careful temperature and time control achieves, the enzymes must be completely destroyed. The prolonged boiling takes care of this.

3) The prolonged boiling sterilises the wort. A dilute sugar and protein solution provides an excellent culture for alien bacteria and moulds to grow on. Without once sterilising the wort, it would never survive the week or so required for fermentation.

4) The long, intensive boiling brings about chemical changes to the protein molecules, causing them to either coagulate into lumps large enough to settle out, or break down into molecules small enough to dissolve or suspend colloidally in the wort. Either way, the wort clears after 1-2 hours boiling. The actual change in chemical nature occurs quite suddenly and it can be observed how the wort from one moment to the next clears. Some

writers describe its appearance as 'shiny'. The boiling process can only be ceased after this so called 'hot break', has occurred.

5) The boiling process also reduces the volume of the wort and so concentrates the wort and allows the brewer to choose his own final alcohol percentage. Home-brewers, assuming that they sparge with due care to the points made in the chapter on this subject, should never end up with a wort volume which exceeds the projected final volume of the beer. Hence the wort volume should need no reduction. This allows the lid to be left on during the boiling phase and much energy saved!

The presence of sugar in the wort causes the boiling point of the water to be raised above 100°C and accelerates the hot break. Any sugar which one intends to add, should be added before the cooking phase, and in order to keep the sugar concentration, and thus the boiling point as high as possible, the overall volume of wort is kept as low as can be managed. Hence the need for effective sparging!

Bringing 15-20 ltr. of wort to the boil can take a long time. Keeping it boiling vigorously is important, as the more the protein particles are swirled around, the better they coagulate. This boiling process can be an energy intensive and time consuming process. The use of an immersion heater allows one to safely insulate the pot with an old wool blanket. This considerably shortens the time required to reach the hot break. Insulating the 25 ltr. saucepan with such a blanket and using a 1.5 kW electric hot plate for heating works well but should be done in a shed away from the house, partly because of the smell of the boiling hops, but also because an insurance company won't give a sympathetic hearing if the blanket and then the house is set on fire during this undertaking!

The pot in which the wort is boiled must have a large cross section to allow for the frothing which sometimes occurs, and give the foam an opportunity to disperse without boiling over. The saucepan should on no account be more than ²⁄₃rds full! If the wort does boil over there is little opportunity to remove the pot quickly from the heat. No rapid movements should be undertaken with 15 kg of boiling water! The sticky charred mess left to be cleaned up afterwards is a sobering lesson in prevention being better than cure.

Müller in his 1845 treatise on brewing, records that English brewers keep most of the protein in mixed wheat and barley malt beers by boiling the wort for 5-8 hours! Under this treatment, the coagulated protein breaks down and is re-dissolved in the wort. This allows (says Müller) a prolonged second fermentation during storage by providing sufficient nutrient for the yeast. Between 9-12 months are required for maturation of such ales and porters, during which time the alcohol content reaches 8-10%. I have included Müller's description in the recipes, although I have found no mention of this method in English literature of the time. Müller was especially impressed by these brews because of the expense involved (presumably in fuel costs) and the disinterested way the English could afford to leave capital idle and depreciating during the long maturation time. Monckton records that porter was stored for up to a year around 1700 although this had been reduced to no more than 2 months by Müller's time. Obviously economic factors had become more important in 19th century England than Müller thought.

The cold break

After boiling one should have a clear wort with 'shine'. During the cooling process the solubility of the proteins in the wort decreases and they begin to precipitate out. This cold haze is less than the hot haze which occurred during coagulation prior to the hot break. If the 'cold break', doesn't occur satisfactorily then the suspended substances can give the beer an unfortunate bitterness as well as a haze. Rapid cooling and stirring help the cold haze to form and precipitate out of the wort. After boiling, the saucepan and contents should be removed from the hotplate to somewhere cool. Remember to ban everyone else from the kitchen during this hazardous undertaking.

Filtering the wort.

The wort has to be filtered one more time in order to remove the hop flowers and any coagulated protein globules. The hop flowers form a very lose filter bed and thus only remove the largest of the coagulated particles. Filtration through a linen cloth spanned across the fermentation butt is very effective but liable to be blocked by the sticky particles, upon which the passage of the wort through the filter virtually ceases. Trial and error with various loosely woven materials is the only solution, but it does help to scoop out the hop flowers from the hopped wort first and lay them on the cloth to form a rough pre-filter. It is important not to leave a slowly filtering wort to its own devices as it will quickly loose its sterility and go off.

Once filtered, the temperature and relative density are measured and the necessary dilution made to produce a wort with the sugar content that will yield the projected final alcohol percentage (see appendix 4). When all this is done, a good working yeast is added to the fermentation butt which is then shut but not sealed.

If you have the fortune to visit a commercial brewery, you will not be able to see the fermentation first hand because it is carried out in sterile rooms. Often enough in the past whole batches of beer had to be destroyed because alien bacteria or 'wild' yeast cells sent the beer sour. Frequent mention is made in historical house-brew literature of 'means of curing a sour beer'. These usually consisted of attempting to neutralise the acid taste with calcium carbonate or something similar. One can't rule out some form of health hazard when sour beers are chemically neutralised, for although the taste may be regulated, the flourishing microbes responsible for the taste and their associated toxins will be little impressed by such gentle treatment. Thus I recommend one quick filtration through a loosely woven cloth and aim at the filtration not taking more than 30 minutes.

Fermentation

As has already been mentioned, there are two types of fermentation available to the brewer but as these require totally different conditions in order to convert the sugar into alcohol, one must have a clear idea what is being aimed at and what conditions and yeast will produce the wished for product. In either case though, a slow second fermentation occurs during maturation.

The two main differences in the fermentation types are the ability of the bottom fermenter to work at temperatures below 10°C and the ability of the top fermenter to occlude the carbon dioxide gas in the yeast particles and thereby lower its density sufficiently to allow it to swim on the surface of the wort.

Top fermenters: Saccharomyces cerevisiae.

These types of yeast work best between 17-20°C. In commercial breweries one often starts the fermentation at around 16°C and slowly raises it to 22°C. The home-brewer may have difficulty in controlling the temperature so carefully and it is not absolutely necessary. On no account should one obey the instructions on the side of home-brew cans, recommending placing the fermentation vat in an airing cupboard and running the fermentation for 3 days at 25°C! This is much too warm and if for any reason the yeast doesn't start fermenting, the wort will have gone off before you notice anything is wrong. The warmer the fermentation, the more side reactions take place and the less pure is the product. This is because higher alcohols, called fusel oil, (Greek — bad spirit) are produced. They do add an additional taste to the drink and to a limited extent are desirable if not necessary, but they are also responsible for the thick heads the next morning.

As soon as possible after boiling, the cooled, filtered and diluted wort is transferred to a plastic fermentation vat which will probably be a white dustbin with a well fitting but not sealed lid. The yeast is added and the vat shut and left. Many home-brewers make a yeast starter about 12 hours before the fermentation is to be commenced and that way they can be sure that they have not been sold a duff yeast sample. In a perfect world, this is sound practice, but if you forget, don't worry, for the dried yeasts currently available in the home-brew shops have become so reliable that I cannot recall one failing. Just stir the dried yeast into the wort. If a starter is to be made, then the yeast is mixed with a little of the wort, or if none is available, with dilute household sugar, and left preferably protected by an air lock, or covered with a cloth. After a few hours the yeast can be seen to be unmistakably working. It is then stirred into the wort when the latter is ready. Provided the temperature of the wort remains around 16-17°C, then within 12 hours a thick mat of yeast foam forms on the surface of the beer. This emulsion of carbon dioxide trapped in yeast and other proteins provides an excellent protection against bacteria and moulds which may ruin the beer. Even so the vat should be opened as little as possible. Once the yeast has used up the oxygen freely available to it, a different type of fermentation starts and produces different taste and aroma components. This process is also hindered by too higher temperature, hence my warning about airing cupboards and haste! If after a day the wort shows no signs of lively fermentation, a new yeast sample should be added. One can also try to start fermentation by raising the temperature, but if this is unsuccessful, then the risk of ruining the wort with wild spores is increased.

This first stage of the fermentation, which involves the yeast using up the available oxygen and about half the sugar to produce new yeast cells, is usually over within 24 hours. The second stage of the fermentation, in which the rest of the sugar is converted to alcohol usually takes about 3-4 days, but can take twice as long if the vat is kept cool. During this second phase carbon dioxide can be seen to effervesce from the body of the liquid which causes the pH to fall still further. This increase in acidity precipitates out hop resins and proteins which form a filthy looking scum on the surface of the brew. As much of this scum as possible should be removed with a soup ladle or something similar, for the hop resins can be very harshly bitter in taste. The mat of yeasty foam must be disturbed as little as possible. Some poor quality dried yeasts produce only a layer of oily bubbles on the surface, and as these offer little protection they may as well be removed with the resin layer. A good yeast throws up an alpine landscape across the surface and any resins can be skimmed off without disturbing the young beer.

At some time during this second fermentation phase, the foamy mat of yeast will disperse. The yeast particles are then swept through the wort by the carbon dioxide gas, but as the evolution of the gas becomes slower, the yeast and protein particles settle to the bottom. As this begins to happen the young beer clears and the relative density should be taken. Remember to spin the hydrometer as it is dropped into the beer for this prevents gas bubbles adhering to the hydrometer bulb and stem, which would encourage it to float higher in the liquid than it should. If the relative density has fallen below 1.010 then the beer is ready for storing.

Bottom fermenters. Saccharomyces Carlsbergensis.

If a bottom fermenting yeast is chosen, the wort is cooled to about 16-18°C and a good, working sample of the yeast stirred into the wort. As soon as the yeast is obviously fermenting, a foam is building and gas evolves, the vat is placed in a cool area. Bottom fermenters should work at about 5-8°C and this means that a shed or outhouse in winter is needed. Because the second phase of the fermentation will take about 10 days, the vat should be well covered to prevent any contamination. By the same token, the low temperature will inhibit the proliferation of any bacteria or fungi. Vats to which an airlock can be fitted are useful, but prevent the hop resins and other precipitations being removed from the surface of the fermenting wort. Such vats are also very difficult to clean after fermentation is finished. After about 8-10 days, the young beer should have a relative density of between 1.010-1.015 and is ready for storing.

Remember, the low temperature and slow fermentation are responsible for steering the taste of the beer in a certain direction. Using a bottom fermenting yeast for a fast fermentation will not produce a good lager or pils, although what you do get may well be easy on the palate.

Maturing and clearing the new beer.

"In the Icelandic sagas beer is frequently referred to, and although the accounts of its manufacture are rather obscure, it is easy to gather that it was drunk very new, a feast always preceded by a brewing as well as a baking, whilst an unsuccessful brew was a terrible misfortune, the king and his court sitting sulkily over their ale, all in a bad humour over the failure of this essential adjunct to their merriment".

(Stopes. 1885)

78

If beer is difficult to keep, don't try; drink it! seems to be the message. But the newly fermented beer does have any number of shortcomings. The hop taste is sometimes harsh, there may be quite a lot of yeast floating in it which has its own flavour, but all of these drawbacks tend to be more a function of what we are used to than any inherent failing of a new brew. Wine producing areas of Germany drink so called 'Federweißen', which is very young wine. It is extremely cloudy and makes one very drunk, but slips down a treat with warm onion cake, its traditional accompanist. Enjoyment of this combination does require a lack of any initial prejudice and I suspect that the same is true of immature beers. As recipes later will show, beer was frequently drunk only a few days old and extremely cloudy. Monckton in his researches discovered an incident in 1449 in which Oxford brewers were in trouble for selling poor ale, and one Richard Bennet undertook to allow his ale to stand at least twelve hours before serving it to the colleges or halls. One wonders if only academics were protected from the rages of young ale or perhaps their consumption was so prolific as to require young beer to be served. Throughout history, students and their professors have never been noted for modest drinking habits.

The normal case though is to syphon the beer out the fermentation vat, leaving excess yeast behind. The beer is left shut from the air, usually in a keg and eventually clears completely. The important word here is eventually! I have never known any beer never clear. The question is how long one is prepared to wait? The second problem, more intractable than drinker's impatience, is that yeast itself goes off and can upset the flavour of the beer. If the yeast decomposes through too longer maturation, the gases produced can split the cask or explode the bottle. There are three ways round such problems.

1) When the beer tastes right, drink it, cloudy or not. You will have learnt enough about the personality of the author by now to know that this is the method I use!

2) The above method can be modified but the beer is filtered before racking for a final time. This is the method favoured by breweries, especially on the Continent, where for the last 50 years, the beer has been filtered through Kieselgur. Luers wrote on this subject, 'filtration serves the purpose of removing the very last haze from the beer, which doesn't naturally precipitate out in the storage keg, and thus satisfies the exaggerated demand of the drinking public for a totally clear beer. The brewer must also carry some blame here for influencing the public into believing that a light beer should be so crystal clear'.

The same author then reels off a list of damages that filtration causes the beer. The natural colour of the beer is reduced, in some dark beers by up to 40%. We are in fact lucky in the UK. We can still buy a good dark beer but the South German Dunkelbiere of today are according to Luers, but weak imitations of former times. Light beers may have become more 'popular', because some breweries, since mechanisation, don't make a good dark beer any more.

Luers further claims that 25% of the total beer ingredient is left in the filter and this detrimentally alters the taste and the head retention properties of the beer. This additional removal of the hop resins and proteins disturbs the biological equilibrium in the beer, which reduces its keeping qualities. If Luers is right, and I'm sure that such an eminent scientist could back up his claims, then we have the irony of removing yeast in order to improve the shelf life, but in so doing, removing the very substances which help the beer keep. This almost certainly is the reason why house brews are far more nutritional and of course have the added advantage of vitamin B_{12} from the yeast, which the brewer has carefully removed in order to sell it for much money in health food shops. The carbon dioxide content is also drastically reduced by filtration and the pH of the final product altered. The only explanation for such wanton vandalism by brewers is that filtering saves storage and equipment being tied up during long maturation.

It must be regarded as a stroke of providential luck that the home-brewer cannot successfully filter his beer! Haze is healthy!

3) We can mix the beer with finings, which are normally gelatine. As the gelatine settles out it encapsulates the yeast and protein and drags it to the bottom too. If the beer is racked carefully a second time, then the finings and yeast can be left behind.

This method is favoured in the UK. Many home brew books, beer kits and I suspect commercial breweries use finings. Vegetarians raise obvious objections to this procedure and as August Ernst Müller wrote in 1845, it really isn't necessary. If he didn't need finings, except for commercial expediency, I don't see why we should today. I quote: "It is most unnecessary to speak on this operation, for with a knowledge of the procedures and rules I have given, it should be simplicity for a brewer to ferment such beers as need no artificial clarification. However one can make mistakes during the cooking of the wort, or somewhere else for that matter, and as a result of which the beer clears only much later, which process oft has a disturbing influence on turnover. The *Hausenblase* (the air bladder of various fish,) which is used for finings, is softened with a wooden hammer and then soaked in water for 18-20 hours. This is then cut into small pieces and soaked in an earthenware pot in a 1:1 mixture of water and wine or a 10:1 mixture of water and a good brandy. The pot is left in a warm place until the solids are dissolved , which usually takes about two days. 2 Loths (approximately 1 oz.) of Hausenblase diluted with 2 ltr. of water and 2 ltr. of wine is sufficient to clear 5-8 buckets of beer. (1 bucket — 36 ltr.). This mixture is stirred into the unclear beer which should then clear within 2-3 days".

He further records, "One can also use parchment dust with calf trotters instead of air bladders", but the normal gelatine finings available in the home brew shop may seem an easier option. Some finings retail under the name 'Isinglass', which is actually a corruption of the Low German word 'Huisenblas' which itself comes from 'Hausenblase'. Thus this method of clearing beer was brought to England in the 16th century by the same Dutch artisans who introduced us to hops.

Gelatine finings can be made by warming gelatine powder in water until dissolved up and then stirring this solution into the beer. After about 3 days the beer clears and may be syphoned off the residue into a clean keg where it is kept until required. The beer may still need time to mature and here the cellar master's taste buds are needed. Experience tells the seasoned publicans when the beer is ready to be served. Strong beers with 8% alcohol will need at least 8 weeks to mature, but many other weaker varieties should be worth sampling after only 4 weeks. If a beer has any unpleasant side taste, it should be left another few weeks. It is amazing how a beer can taste like medicine after 4 weeks, but harvest great praise 2 weeks later. Once a beer is ready, it should be drunk within a relatively short time as it will only retain its highest quality for about 4 weeks, and then begin to deteriorate. If malt of doubtful quality has been used, it is worth trying a beer fairly regularly in case it doesn't keep at all well. Bottom fermented beers should always be kept at least 8 weeks before testing.

Cool storage of the beer assists clearing, bottom fermenters being kept as low as 2°C. Bottled beers settle out faster than keg beers but will take as long to mature. If you want to get a clear beer ready quickly, then mature it in bottles. I always let the beer mature properly and then serve it in stone tankards if it isn't quite clear.

Nowadays, with most beer filtered by the brewery and sold from pressurised kegs, a fairly standardised beer is always available. The publican's instinct is no longer required to decide when the beer is ready. Today's quality control is "is it clear?" If so, it is ready! On the continent, where bottled beers are still most popular, the beer undergoes a haphazard final maturation, usually on a warm supermarket shelf. The maturation actually lasts until it is bought and drunk.

Although August Müller's adventures with swim-bladders and calf's trotters may seem a bit over the top for us today, don't be put off his brewing recipes in Chapter 9 for he had some fine beers to offer.

Kegging the beer.

The maturation of the beer usually takes place in a keg. The beer is either sold and served from the keg, or in some cases re-filled into bottles. The point here is that if too much sugar is still present in the young beer, as the yeast continues to work, the pressure of carbon dioxide in the keg or bottle will cause the container to explode. This can be most humorous, like the time a friend of mine was woken in the early hours of the morning by a series of explosions and came into the parlour to find the cat trembling and soaked with beer in the corner. However the cat, nor the landlady saw the funny side of the incident! On a more serious note, do remember that explosions of carbonated drink bottles, especially those of home brew, have caused terrible injury to unsuspecting drinkers. I have had two narrow escapes which only cost me a re-decoration of the room I was in at the time!

"La bière sauvage" or "Wild-Werden des Bieres".

"Savage beers given to becoming wild without provocation", is an apt description which unfortunately the English language cannot parallel. The sin and error of bottling or casking a beer with too high relative density, i.e. too high residual sugar content, may not always cause an explosion but can lead to a fire extinguisher effect when the bottle or keg is opened. Kegs should never explode as they are all fitted with pressure release valves which prevent a gas pressure build up in excess of the breaking strain of the barrel. Bottles are a different matter. Here are a few tips on how to avoid an accident.

1) Don't bottle a beer until the relative density is below 1.006.

2) Don't bottle a beer on a cold winter's day and then open the bottle after it has been standing in a warm place. Care is always needed when opening a winter beer in warm weather.

3) If you suspect a bottle of possible treachery, always wrap a strong linen cloth around the bottle and hold it away from the face.

4) If you find a long forgotten bottle then treat it circumspectly especially if there is a lot of yeast sediment present. The yeast may have simply gone off and in so doing decomposed to gaseous products.

5) Always fill bottles to their correct capacity. The gas can exert far greater force on the walls of a half filled bottle, than it can a full one.

Remember: while the gas is dissolved in the beer, the bottle won't explode. The gas only exerts a force as it comes out of solution. The less room it has, the less can come out of solution; until you open the bottle that is...!

6) Priming sugar is I believe the cause of 99% of home brew accidents. Some home brewers allow their worts to ferment out completely in the fermentation vat. At least they think they do but a check with a hydrometer would show there to be some residual slow fermenting dextrines still in the new beer and just because the fermentation appears to be finished they assume it has. They then bottle the beer, and in order to achieve a head on the beer, put a spoonful of (priming) sugar in each bottle in order to produce a little bit more carbon dioxide. There is nothing inherently wrong with this practice provided:

   – the main fermentation really has finished and there is not more sugar still present than appears.

   – only one level teaspoon of priming sugar per litre of beer is added.

German breweries are of course forbidden to add a little sugar to help the carbon dioxide formation during maturation and so they take a fresh sample of malt extract and add that. How noble?

Traditionally beers were always served virtually flat, the only gas present being that which naturally dissolves in the liquid at that temperature. This is a most satisfactory method as no explosion can occur. All excess carbon dioxide is free to escape. As the beer is usually made and stored at below room temperature, and served cool, bubbles will be slowly discharged from the beer as it warms during drinking in a warm room. Such a brew is most recommendable. The problem is that beer served in this way from a barrel will immediately begin to go off for in order to run the beer from the barrel, air must be allowed to enter through some other orifice. The beer soon deteriorates in air. The solution to

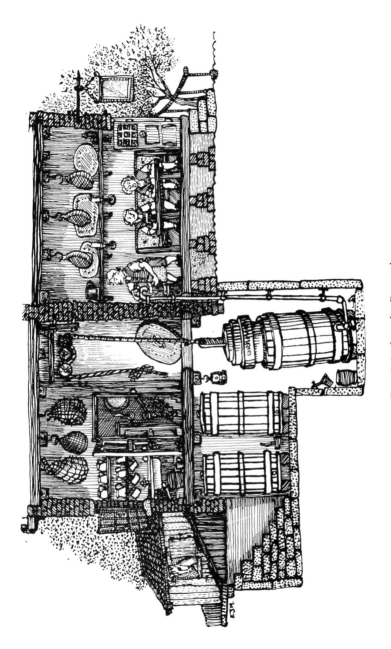

A Beer Machine by Bramah.

this was to drink the beer within one or at the most two days, and when barrels were small this was not a problem. With the improvement of machine tools, elaborate pumps were made which allowed the beer to be run out without letting air in. The breweries later solved the problem by keeping the beer in large kegs under an artificially introduced blanket of carbon dioxide, and as beer is drawn off, more gas is injected to compensate for the change in volume. This way the barrel may be emptied at leisure without ever allowing air to contact the beer. This principle is used by the makers of the plastic kegs available from home brew shops and works very well. Injecting carbon dioxide into the barrel does create an artificial head, but provided only very little is injected and no great pressure allowed to build up in the barrel during the storage fermentation, a nearly flat traditional beer can be achieved. Bottling cold without priming sugar will also work, as will storage in non-pressurised floppy plastic containers which, rather like some camper's water holders, collapse as the water is run out.

Before plastic or lined steel barrels, oak was the main material used for beer containers and still is in some breweries. It is so expensive now that only the large stationary storage vats are of wood. In the past these and the smaller delivery barrels were often sealed with tar on the inside and this was a skilled job if the beer was not to take on any taste. Some were not sealed as the slow exchange of air through the wood (breathing) produced beers with their own special qualities.

Finally on this subject it must be noted that storage in bottles requires a special pouring technique to be applied. In order not to disturb the yeast mat, which should have formed as a sediment in the bottom of the bottle, the beer is more decanted into glasses than poured. Enough glasses must be ready and then the bottle is opened and emptied in one draught, without returning the bottle to the vertical before it is empty. In this way the yeast should remain undisturbed. Should some yeast get into the glass then the problem is more optical than one of taste. Provided the yeast is only present in small amounts, the taste will not alter.

Top fermenting beers, of moderate starting density, should be finished in about 6-8 weeks, stronger beers require much longer, sometimes 12 months. All bottom fermenters require several months. This is because in lagers and strong beers up to 40% of the total sugar is polysaccharides which can only be slowly dealt with by the yeast. Less strong top fermenters contain only 25% dextrine. The beers are finished when the remaining sugar has been converted to alcohol and carbon dioxide, the latter being responsible for the head on the beer. Thus a small amount of fermentable material in the young beer is essential for a successful brew.

8. Malting at Home.

"A Man would do nothing, if he waited until he could do it so well that no one would find fault with what he has done".

(*Cardinal Newman.*)

After seven chapters of theory and chat around the subject, there is no excuse left for not getting on with making some malt. Before starting though it is worth gathering all the necessary equipment. Once the barley is under way it won't wait till tomorrow.

The equipment.

1) Scales or balance.
   One must be able to weigh at least 10 kg., which many kitchen scales won't manage. A beam balance or sliding weight scales are best. Neither are cheap. Your local angling shop may be able to supply an alternative in the form of a simple spring balance. (More correctly called a 'Newton meter'.)

2) 2 × 10 ltr. buckets with lids.
   The more buckets and containers one has in the brewing and malting kitchen the better, so two buckets may only be considered a minimum number. They should be identical in size and shape, so when they are pressed one in the other they give a tight fit. Test them to see if they are airtight by pouring a little water into the gap between the buckets. Perforate one bucket's base with about 100 × 6 mm. holes to form a sieve.

3) 35 ltr. Container.
   Home-brew shops sell white plastic fermentation vats, which though advertised as 5 gallon, in fact hold more and are ideal. Whatever is used, it must have a good fitting but not airtight lid for later use as a fermentation vat.

4) Wooden frame.
   This can be quickly nailed together from any unwanted wood. Its purpose is to allow the sieve-bucket (2) to be hung to drain into the large container (3).

5) A litre measuring jug.
   Many buckets are calibrated in litres and would do instead.

6) Thermometer.
   0-100°C range is required.

7) Wire baskets.
   Galvanized wire mesh baskets must be constructed to fit whatever oven or warm air chamber is to be used to dry the malt. The mesh should be about 3

mm^2 and can be bought in good iron mongers. I have also purchased perforated zinc sheet by the roll which is just as good. Three trays 50×25 cm^2 in size, are required to dry green malt from 2.5 kg. dry barley. This is 3750 cm^2 drying surface. If one constructs a cabinet, (appendix 6) then a much larger surface area should be aimed at for future convenience.

8) Aquarium pump and water circulator.
A cheap aquarium pump will do. The water circulator is slightly more difficult but inexpensive and obtainable from specialist tropical fish shops. The principle is that air is pumped to the bottom of the container, then rises up a plastic tube. In so doing it lifts and circulates water from the bottom of the bucket, aerating it on the way.

9) Notebook and marker pen.
A notebook for immediately recording weighings is essential. A marker pen for writing on the sides of the buckets is most useful. Much time can be saved if the weight of the empty bucket is clearly visible on the side of that bucket, written with indelible pen. This weight is called the 'tare'.

10) Oven or drying chamber.
Think carefully how the green malt is to be dried.
Temperatures below 40°C must be maintained for several days. Air must be able to circulate around the wire baskets (7). A design for a malt and hop drying chamber is described in appendix 6.

A basic recipe for making malt.

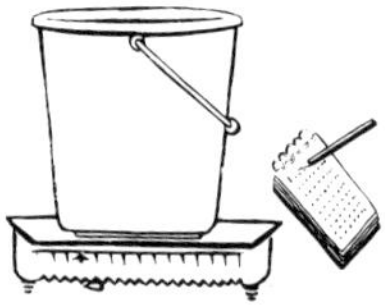

A

1) The steep.

Brewers' barley is to be soaked for 72 hours in water. At least 1.5 ltr. of water will be needed to compensate for the liquid absorbed by the barley. This must be allowed for or added within a few hours. The temperature of the water should be 8-10°C.

A Weigh the buckets and write their weights clearly on their sides in indelible pen.

B ⅔ fill a bucket with fresh cold water and sprinkle 2.5 kg. of barley on the surface. The barley soon sinks, leaving any dirt and straw floating. The latter can be carefully removed.
The original mass of the barley and the tares of the buckets (2) must be noted.

B

2) Temperature and aeration of the steep.

The steep water should never exceed 10°C. In warm weather the water may need cooling in a fridge. As the steep temperature should remain below 12°C the whole steep process may need to be carried out in one of the salad trays of a fridge or in a cool outhouse or cellar.

In order to prevent suffocation of the barley, change the

steep water frequently. The first change should be after about 2, and thereafter every 12 hours.

C The wet malt is heavy and to allow it to drain properly during steep water changes, hang the sieve bucket (2) in the large container (3) using the wooden frame (4).

After the 2 hour water change, the water changes may be reduced to once daily by aerating the water continually. This not only reduces the work, but saves valuable starch being washed from the grains and shortens the time needed to malt, by several days.

D To this end, air is pumped to the bottom of the steep bucket using a cheap aquarium pump with a water circulator attachment (8).

C

D

3) Properties of steeped malt.

After 72 hours in the steep, the barley is soft and easily squashed. It can be dissected with the fingernail. The broken open corn writes on a rough surface rather like chalk and the water content has risen to 45% of the total weight. The volume will have risen commensurately, the grains have a swollen appearance and if an aerated steep has been employed, small white root tips may already be visible.

The mass of the steeped grain should be 3.6 kg. and towards the end of the steep it is worth frequently checking the mass as the steep may be considered finished when a 45% water content has been reached. Unnecessarily prolonged steeping is bad for the grain! 4.5 kg. of dry barley will weigh 7.6 kg. after the steep and this is probably the most that home maltsters can handle bearing in mind that this mass may need 2 days to dry.

4) Germination.

When the steep is finished, the wet barley is allowed to drain thoroughly. This is done using the sieve bucket (2) and wooden frame (4). After draining, the wet barley is left in the sieve bucket.

Conditions for germination.

Germination takes several days and during this time the corn must not be allowed to dry out. If the barley is thought to be drying out, check carefully the mass of the barley (hence the reason for noting the tare of the bucket) as the barley may still be absorbing its own surface moisture. Sprinkling the barley with water is very bad practice and should never be necessary if a cool, damp atmosphere is provided. Furthermore, the corn respires, using atmospheric oxygen and releasing carbon dioxide. As in all biological processes, there are a thousand things which can happen and the conditions which will optimize the desired process are important.

– A temperature in the body of the germinating mass of between 12°C and 15°C is required and no part of the germinating barley may exceed 20°C.

– The germination is carried out in a dark room which should be at about 10°C. Again here a fridge may be used.

– The heap of wet grain is turned as often as possible in order to let fresh air in and built up heat escape.

– The time required for germination depends on the temperature of the heap but as a good malster attends his heap regularly he recognizes when the green malt is finished.

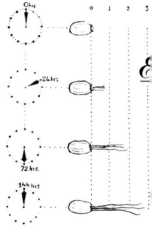

Germination takes place in two phases which are clearly recognisable. In the first three days after the steep the grains show the tips of their roots, rather like eyes. After three days the acrospire is so large as to cause the husk to swell slightly and careful observation of the progress of the swelling gives the best measure of when the green malt is ready for drying. The vigour of the barley's growth is strongest during this first phase, producing the most respiration products. The metabolism slows somewhat in the second phase, roots are formed and these mat themselves making turning more difficult but even more important. The green malt is finished when the acrospire has reached ⅔ the length of the grain.

6) Germinator

A simple Germinator makes life much easier during the first phase. Two identical buckets (2) pushed inside each other to form a tight fit. The inner bucket with the perforated base holds the wet steeped malt. Air is pumped into a few inches of water contained in the lower bucket using the aquarium pump. 1 ltr./minute of air is adequate and so the cheapest pump is sufficient. The water saturated air serves several purposes.

– It prevents the steeped barley drying out.

– It sweeps out carbon dioxide gas which can otherwise build up and suffocate the barley.

– Because the water is being evaporated by the air movement through it, the air is cooled and prevents heat build up in the heap.

Without a germinator the mass of barley will need to be turned several times per day. In this case the barley must be tipped out of its germinating bucket, (the sieve bucket), thoroughly turned and then returned. The sieve bucket (2) is hung using the wooden frame (4) in the large container (3) during germination, as the holes in the bucket will allow the heavier carbon dioxide gas to escape, thus drawing fresh air in the top. Although the sieve bucket is covered during germination the lid must not prevent this natural circulation. The advantage of a germinator is that the barley need only be turned once or in warm weather perhaps twice a day.

Provided an aerated steep and germinator have been used, the white roots are visible after three days, and the first phase is finished. If aeration hasn't been used then the barley won't be so far advanced. In either case, phase two begins after 72 hours.

7)   Second phase.

For the second germination phase, the germinating barley in the sieve bucket (2) is suspended in the wooden frame in the manner described above. The lid should fit well so that now the escape of the heavy carbon dioxide gas is hindered. This slows down the respiration of the barley but the enzyme production continues. (Carbon dioxide bath.)

However:

– the grain may appear to sweat and if it is allowed to retain too much surface water, mould will start to grow.

– the grain must not be killed off by suffocation. Some air must still be able to get in.

The grain must be turned so often that:

– water and heat accumulation are prevented. The temperature should not rise above 15°C. 20°C is an absolute maximum. Even at 20°C there is a risk that the grain acrospire will "shoot", and the malt be ruined.

– the roots don't form an impenetrable felt which will make drying most difficult.

– grain suffocation is prevented.

Turning once a day is sufficient to break up the root mat but may not suffice to prevent heat build up.

If a germinator has not been used, then the second phase is merely a continuation of the first, except that the grain is not turned as often, and air circulation generally decreased.

8)   Drying the green malt.

The germinated barley is called "green malt". The green malt grains should have acrospires which are about ⅔ the length of the grains. It may be necessary to open a few husks in order to identify the acrospire, but once recognised, its length can be accurately ascertained by simply inspecting a handful of green malt grains. The magic ⅔ is of course only an average and there will be a fair distribution of lengths either side of this figure.

The bar chart (see overleaf) of acceptable acrospire lengths shows that some malt types can tolerate much more developed acrospires without detriment.

Green malt has a water content of around 30% so our original 2.5 kg. barley now weighs 3.7 kg. Kiln drying the green malt below 45°C reduces the water

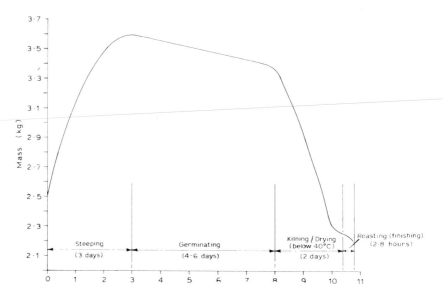

content without destroying the enzymes. Only when the water content of the malt has fallen below 8%, can the temperature be raised. As much as 2 days may be required to dry the malt.

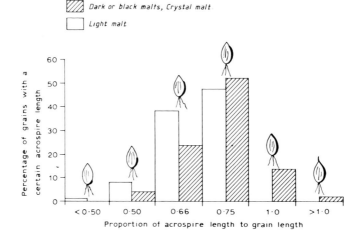

The higher temperatures give the malt its special qualities required for a certain type of beer. If the temperature is raised too soon, the malt flour is no longer white and chalky, but hard and glassy. Such malt is only suitable for conversion into dark malt used for giving colour to the beer.

Different methods of kilning malt.

Instinctively one reaches for the baking oven for drying malt but there are few ovens which will maintain the low temperature required. Ovens with an air circulation fan may be suitable but the length of drying will present problems in the kitchen.

Normally one can find a warm airy chamber somewhere in the house and then the green malt can be spread thinly (2 cm.) on the wire trays (7) and left to its own devices. The chamber must be dark to prevent photosynthesis starting and the grains must dry sufficiently quickly to prevent further growth of the acrospire. If the acrospires or roots still show signs of life after about 6 hours of drying, then the air circulation is insufficient, usually solved by spreading the green malt more thinly. More rarely the temperature is too low. The door of a baking oven often needs to be slightly ajar for the initial drying phase to allow ample circulation.

The temperature of the drying malt should be frequently checked. During the initial phase, when a lot of water is evaporating, the temperature of the malt will probably remain anything up to 10°C less than the ambient temperature in the oven. As the water content drops, so the malt temperature gets closer to the oven or drying chamber temperature. When the malt has reached the ambient temperature it is probably nearly dry. The mass must be checked by weighing the malt and trays and the percentage water calculated, (see appendix 3) but the experienced malster will quickly recognise when the malt is ready for roasting.

9)   Finishing the Malt: Roasting.

Once dried, the pale malt is either stored or converted to a darker malt type by roasting the pale malt at higher temperatures for varying lengths of time. Mixing these darker malts allows the manifold variety of beers to be brewed. The exact conditions required for a particular malt are given in the recipes below which enable the once most common English and Continental types to be made.

Unlike the initial drying phase, exact temperature control is not needed for roasting and a standard baking oven is quite adequate. The layers of malt must however be kept to 2 cm. if a uniform product is to be achieved. If this is not considered important, then thicker layers may be roasted.

Malt types and their roasting temperatures.

The kilning curves provide an approximate guide to how the temperature varies as kilning progresses. The square shaped curves describe the oven temperature for a particular malt batch. The gentle curves however are the temperatures in the malt itself, only rising slowly to the oven temperature as water is lost. The two types of curve must be viewed and used independently of each other.

Pale or Bohemian (see charts overleaf).

These are the most common types of malt because they are very gently dried

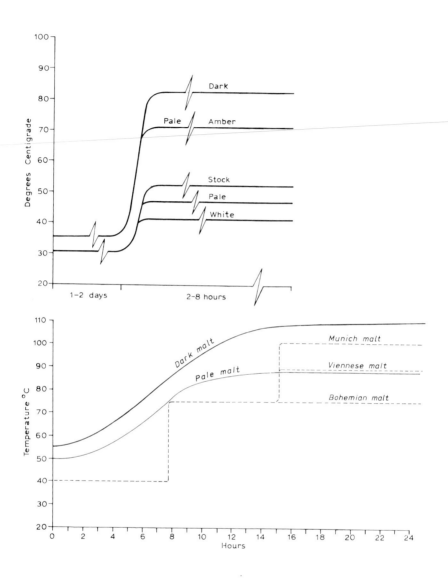

at less than 45° thus affording maximum protection for the enzymes and producing the best extract yield during mashing. After complete drying the malt is given a quick 2.5 hour "roast", at about 55-70°C in order to give the Czechoslovakian Bohemian malt. 8 hours at 80-110°C produces Pale Malt.

Bohemian malt makes the typical Pils or Lager beer. Pale malt is the English equivalent but is a good deal darker than the Bohemian, being roasted some

30°C higher. It is the main representative for infusion recipes, the Bohemian enjoying the more complicated decoction process.

The less common "white malt", used to be finished between 35-40°C, i.e. not roasted at all.

By varying the roasting temperatures and times, one can produce one's own individual "House Malt".

2)   Dark Malts.

Brewers who live in an area with temporary hard water will need a darker malt to bring the pH of the mash down. The malt is dried initially as for pale malt and then roasted for about 10 hours at 100-105°C for a Munich malt or 85-90°C to produce the Viennese variety. English dark malts were traditionally treated at lower temperatures. Ford in 1862 recommended 76-88°C but gives no times for finishing but it must have been many hours. True dark malts frequently cannot be bought in home-brew shops. Crystal malt, which provides more colour is mixed with paler sorts but this does not produce the same beer as that brewed from a true dark malt.

Imperial malt has disappeared into brewing history but is easily made by finishing pale malt at 120-135°C for several hours.

3)   Golden or Amber Malt.

English amber malt, which was made on the Continent under the name "golden malt", cannot be purchased as it also seems to be one of the casualties of breweries concentrating on a few popular beer types. It used to be used for mild, brown ales, porters and stouts which it gave a "brown head", to or instead of dark malt in the South German dark beers. It was superceded by the more economical brown and black malts. It is more difficult to make then dark malt and yields less extract than the latter. The temperature diagram shown must be closely adhered to. It is essentially pale malt finished at 70°C.

4)   Crystal or Caramel Malt.

Gently coloured beers are usually nowadays made by mixing crystal or "Kara-melmalz", with pale malt. These malts supply colour and taste but little extract. Trying to replace dark malts with crystal malt significantly alters the taste of the beer. The high drying temperature (65°C) destroys the enzymes and provides for a dark glassy malt which is then finished off at 130°C.

5)   Black Malt.

The Bavarians have long made very dark beers which cannot be produced by dark malts alone. Thus they mixed 1 − 5% black malt into their standard pale Munich malt.

Black malt is fairly briskly dried at 80°C but then roasted at 160-170°C. The maltings use slowly revolving drums, rather like coffee roasters, in order to work at these temperatures and achieve a uniform product as well as preventing burning against the hot metal parts. Stopes produced the apparatus already mentioned to make black malt and claims to have sold it very successfully to Bavarian brewers.

To make black malts in a baking oven, the malt must be spread very thinly and turned occasionally but even so a fair amount of smoke is unavoidable.

Stout and porter are made using a small amount of black malt but the extract is obviously low.

Black malt should be used immediately after roasting.

Esoteric malts.

6) Brown, Blown, Snap or Porter Malt.

I doubt anyone has made this malt commercially in the UK in the last 100 years, but beer made from a similar malt is brewed and most sought after around the area of Nuremberg and Bamberg in Germany. It trades under the names of *Schlenkela*, and *Rauchbier*, respectively. Stopes gives a description of its manufacture in Bishop's Stortford in 1870 which is summarised thus:

"Usually in its preparation, steeping couching and growing are conducted in the ordinary way. Some malsters give a little less time on the withering floor. (Gentle drying phase.) The corn is then laden on the kiln at a thickness rarely exceeding 1½ inches. The fire consists exclusively of wood, generally of oak, but occasionally of beech. Billet and faggott wood are used. Great skill and care are required to tend the fire and turn the floor. This is done only once and the whole drying is completed in 1 to 2 hours. Moderate heat is maintained at first until the moisture has been largely dissipated, then the fire is made up, and flares and blazes so that no little danger exists of the corn igniting. This renders the work of the kiln man both risky and laborious. The sudden and intense heat causes all the grain which has been properly grown to swell to the extent of 25%, and the nature of the fuel employed communicates very agreeably the empyreumatic properties that distinguish this class of malt".

Another description comes closer to the current German technique. The malt is half dried and sprinkled with water which if left about 12 hours, toughens the skin. The corn is spread on wire trays to a depth of 1-2 inches and fired over beech turning at least every four minutes.

7) Wheat Malt.

In the 18th century, Childs considered wheat to be the only corn worth malting. Nowadays only a few German beers are made with this grain. Because wheat has no tough husk, it takes up water far faster than barley and so the steep must be considerably shortened, aerated and stopped as soon as the correct mass increase has been obtained. The acrospire is allowed to grow to twice the length of the corn in order to allow the extra proteins present in wheat to be broken down. According to Dreverhof this process is assisted by spreading the steeped grain very thinly and allowing the hook shaped roots to form a dense felt. Attempting to turn wheat green malt damages the unprotected acrospire. The green malt is dried as barley but the roasting phase carried out over many hours, at temperatures around 80°C.

An anonymous 18th century publican and brewer however recommended malting wheat in the same way as barley, in order to produce "a strong, heady, nourishing, well tasting and fine liquor, which is now more practised than ever".

8) Oat Malt.

Wherever oat beer is mentioned in the literature it receives great praise. I have not successfully brewed an oat ale yet but will keep trying. According to Watkins, oat malt is made exactly as white or pale barley malt. Stopes says oats are easily malted and our anonymous publican wrote, "oats, malted as barley is, will make a weak, soft pleasant drink".

Oats can tend to give impure fermentation products but the higher alcohols such as butanol or butyric acid that may be produced, have such a pungent smell (of rancid butter in the latter case) that one is unlikely to proceed if things have gone wrong. As a rule of thumb, discard any malting or mash if bubbles of unspecified gas rise in the absence of yeast and remember, toxins are not killed by boiling, so it is not safe to say, "the wort will be sterilised so its safe to use suspect ingredients".

9) Roasted Barley.

Unmalted brewers' barley can be roasted at about 200°C and used instead of the black or amber colouring malts. The beer tastes quite different but totally acceptable. It is much less work to make and creates less smoke in the kitchen than black malt.

10) Rice Malt.

Rice can only be malted if a sample with the husk and testa still intact can be obtained. Rice bought in the U.K. has invariably been roughly treated and will not germinate. Rice is high in starch with less gluten than many other grasses and so is easy to brew with. A sample of barley malt is needed to supply the enzymes to break down the starch.

The Japanese do not germinate the rice in order to make rice malt. The cleaned rice is steamed until gelatinized and then worked to a paste. When cooled to around 28-30°C the spores of a fungus called *eurotium oryzae* are mixed in small proportion with the mass which is kept in heaps in the dark at around 26°C. The heap temperature rises to around 30°C. The changes brought about by this treatment are nearly the same as produced by European malting. This Japanese malt has its greatest diastic power at 54°C and so cool mashing is needed around this temperature. The whole story depends though on finding a sample of the correct fungus spores which seems unlikely hence the advice to use a sample of good malt to help supply the enzymes.

11) Rye Malt.

Rye malt is most problematic, tending more than oats to produce butyric fermentation. The butanol isomers are varyingly poisonous but the microbes producing butryfication should never be messed with (cf. oat malt). For this reason rye was historically only malted in times of hardship. It doesn't sound a good tip.

Storing Malt.

Pale, dark and amber malts need to be stored at least four weeks before brewing may commence. All malt is hydroscopic. A finished malt has a water content of less than 4% and this may not be allowed to rise above 6% during storage or the malt becomes "slack", and is only then suitable for converting into black malt. Nowadays plastic bags make slack malt a rarity and are excellent for storage purposes.

Cleaning the malt.

Before the malt may be used, the roots must be removed. This is a tiresome job and is best done immediately after roasting when the roots are most brittle. Simply rubbing handfuls of grain on a flat surface seems most effective, unless you possess a pebble polisher such as are used by lapidaries.

9. Historical Beer Recipes.

"Ask ten brewers and get eleven opinions". *(Old Swiss brewer's proverb.)*

Brewing apparatus.

This list assumes that most of the apparatus for malting (chapter 8) has been obtained. To summarise one should already have:

1) Scales or balance.
2) 2 × 10 ltr. buckets with lids. 1 × 10 ltr. bucket fitted with a false wire bottom covering a tap. (12)
3) 35 ltr. Container.
4) Wooden frame.
5) A litre measuring jug.
6) Thermometer. 0-100°C.   7)   Wire baskets.*
8) Aquarium pump and water circulator.*
9) Notebook and marker pen.
10) Oven or drying chamber.*
    * denotes equipment only required for malting.

In addition is needed:

11) A means of grinding the malt.

    Various options have been discussed. Remember that the malt grains must be broken, not reduced to flour.

12) A mash tub.

    This may be any bucket which can be insulated to prevent heat loss. A 10 ltr. bucket stood in a hot water bath (large saucepan) which is occasionally warmed on the stove, or a bucket wrapped in an old blanket are options. Even better is a bucket stood in a larger bucket, the cavity between them being filled with old rags, or vermiculite etc. If you decide on the water bath idea, you will need to stand the plastic bucket on some pieces of wood. The bucket base may otherwise melt when the water is being warmed on the stove and it is directly against the hot metal.

    If you are prepared to spend money, then a plastic cold box such as is used by campers, is a good solution.

    Whatever is chosen, a temperature drop of not more than 2°C per hour should be aimed at.

    For recipes involving the decoction method, a water bath type set up is indispensable. A second bucket with a tap fitted will also be required. For this a brass tap and connecting piece are mounted through a hole of the correct size which has been drilled through the side of the bucket as far down as possible. The seal between the bucket and tap flange can be made with PTFE tape. A wire mesh with holes not exceeding 3 mm^2 will need to be fitted on the inside of the bucket over the tap outlet, to prevent the tap blocking.

13) pH-paper. 3-7 range.

Many manage without pH-paper and if it is all that is missing from your equipment then start without it.

14) Hydrometer and measuring cylinder.

15) Wooden spoon.

Do not use one that has been used for normal cooking as this will have traces of fat on it which will ruin head retention.

16) Electric hot plate.

17) Old blanket.

18) Filters.

These will be colanders or pieces of nylon stocking, stockinette etc. which can be suspended over the fermentation bucket (3).

19) Plastic syphon tubing.

At least 1.5 m will be required and the correct diameter is available from home-brew shops.

20) Plastic pressure barrel (25 ltr.).

Or an equivalent number of screw-top bottles.

21) Selection of plastic funnels.

22) Large saucepan and lid.

The capacity should be at least 20 ltr. 25-30 ltr. is best.

Brewing.

The quantities and values given in beer recipes can only be approximate. The actual conditions which are achieved depend on the quality and type of malt and the brew water available. Descriptions such as "dark malt", or "hard water", cover a multitude of sins. Unlike baking a cake, if you get things about right, you'll get a drinkable (and probably excellent) product. Thus if a recipe suggests 4 ltr. of water, prepare 5-6 ltr., in case more is required to regulate the mash temperature quickly. The aim though when mashing is to get a thick porridge of the right temperature. Temperature values must be carefully adhered to if you want the beer described. Other values may alter the dextrine/maltose ratio and produce a different beer. Who knows how accurately old brewers checked their temperatures though? They didn't even have the means to measure them! Much above 70°C is certainly bad news for the enzymes although one tended in the past to mash much hotter than now! I give the recipe value and leave it to the brewer to choose a lower temperature if he/she wishes. Don't forget that the strike temperature must be higher than the required mash temperature.

Hop quantities are Hobson's choice. Unless you have an exact analysis of the hops there is no way of really knowing what you are adding. Such an analysis is readily available for hop concentrates. Some hop quantities seem enormous for our present day tastes but after the initial shock one soon learns to love strongly hopped beers. If you live in a high temporary hardness area, and intend to put in large quantities of hops, you may wish to soften all the water to be used in the brew, including the sparge water as carbonate hardness brings out hop harshness.

The sparge quantities which are recommended should be sufficient provided the sparge is efficient. The efficiency of the mash and sparge will determine the amount of extract which is actually obtained and hence the amount and strength of the beer. The values given are based on an expected 80% mash efficiency. Checks with a hydrometer will indicate if more or less water is required in the final dilution. If no household sugar is used, then considerably less dilution will be necessary.

The beer recipes split into two groups. The first are the English brews which use the much simpler infusion method. The second are for the German beers which are far more complicated, using the decoction process. Each group of recipes are preceded by one or more basic methods, and only the varying parameters are then given. There are many books on the market which give step by step idiot proof methods of brewing English beers. If in doubt, then you could learn to brew some simple beers using such books and return to this one in a few months time. Personally I'm for ploughing on regardless. Nothing can really go wrong provided the standard rules of kitchen hygiene are observed.

Basic recipe for a light ale using the infusion method.

Ingredients.

Water	7 ltr. well boiled if temporary hard.
Malt	2.5 kg. pale.
Hops	120-150 g. Hallertauer or Goldings.
Yeast	Top fermenter.

Method.
i)   Mill the malt.

ii)   Put 4 ltr. of the water at 73°C in the mash tub. (12)

iii)   Stir in the milled malt and bring the temperature of the mash as quickly as possible to 65°C.

iv)   Check the pH of the mash. It should be 5.2 − 5.5. If outside this range read the chapter on "water", and appendix 1 before next brewing.

v)   Insulate the mash tub and leave to stand for 3 hours.

vi)   After one hour remove a few drops of the mash and add a few drops of iodine water. There should be no colour change. If there is, then stir

	well, check the temperature and test again after another 30 minutes. A purple/blue colour indicates that the starch has not yet been fully converted to sugar. Experience obviates this step.
vii)	Stir and check the temperature frequently. Adjust it if it has fallen below 63°C by adding with stirring, aliqots of boiling water.
viii)	After 3 hours filter the wort through a colander or piece of nylon held over the fermentation vat by several clothes pegs. (18) Some recipes require the malt to be mashed a second time. If this is the case, put the first wort in a cool place and re-mash the draff.
ix)	Sparge the draff with 10 ltr. water at about 70°C. Check that the last drops of sparge water have no marked taste.
x)	Transfer the wort to a large saucepan (22) and bring it to the boil.
xi)	Add the hops and boil for 1 hour. Remember to keep some of the hops back to add during the boiling. The wort must be boiled for at least 15 minutes after the last hop addition and until it appears to have cleared.
xii)	After 1 hour check the hot break has occurred and then cool the wort as quickly as possible.
xiii)	Filter the wort again to remove the hop remains. Wash any wort from the hop remains with cold water.
xiv)	The wort should be in the fermentation vat. Add 1kg sugar and stir well. Check the density with a hydrometer and adjust the density to 1.045 g/cm^3.
xv)	Add 30 g. of a good working top fermenting yeast and stand at about 17°C until the density has sunk to 1.006 g/cm^3.
xvi)	During the fermentation remove any solids or hop-resin which come to the surface.
xvii)	When fermentation has ceased and the young beer begins to clear, clean the bottles or barrel with a disinfectant sold for the purpose by home-brew shops.
xviii)	Syphon the beer into the bottles/barrel taking care not to disturb the yeast cake at the bottom of the fermentation vat.
xix)	Add priming sugar if this is intended.
xx)	Keep the beer 4-6 weeks in a cool place. Sample the beer after this time. If dissatisfied then keep another 2 weeks and test again. Wait until it is right.
xxi)	If it tastes right but isn't clear, then serve it in stone mugs.

ENGLISH RECIPES.

The basic recipe given above should produce a pale ale, although rather strongly hopped by modern standards. If the same recipe is applied to the following ingredients and parameters, a rich variety of beers can be obtained.

Remember that the term "starting gravity", refers to the density of the diluted wort before fermentation starts.

a) DARK BITTER.

Ingredients:

Malt	1.5 kg. pale.
	1.5 kg. dark.
Hops	120 g. Hallertauer.
Water	5 ltr. moderately hard.
Sugar	1 kg.
Yeast	30 g. top fermenter.

Conditions:

Mash temperature	63°C.
Mash time	4 hours.
Starting gravity	1.040 g/cm^3.
Storage time	6 weeks.
Expected volume	20 ltr.
Alcohol content	5.5%

One can vary this recipe by taking 2.5 kg. of pale malt and 500 g. of crystal malt, both of which can be readily purchased in good home-brew shops.

ALE RECIPES.

Although historically speaking ales refer to unhopped beer, the name has long since lost this original meaning. Pale and brown "ales", are brewed nowadays without any special connotation. These "ale", recipes are from the last two centuries and are all top fermented infusion brews.

Watch out for the hop quantities! I give the amounts from the original recipes. These amounts used in very hard carbonate water will take off the cheek cells like wallpaper stripper.

b) BURTON ALE. 1880.

Ingredients:

Malt	2.5 kg. pale.
Water	5 ltr. per mash, hard but boiled.
Adjuncts	pinch of calcium sulphate
Hops	240 g. Kentish such as Goldings.
Sugar	1 kg.
Yeast	30 g. top fermenter.

Conditions:

Mash temperature	68°C.
Mash time	2.5 hours.

The wort is drained off and then the draff mashed for a second time.

Mash temperature	73°C.
Mash time	1.5 hours.
Sparge volume	12 ltr.
Hop boiling time	2 hours
Initial gravity	1.044 g/cm³.
Storage time	6 weeks.
Expected volume	15-20 ltr.
Alcohol content	6%.

The above recipe is by the Victorian brewer Amsinck. He tells that his teacher 20 years earlier had still brewed to an original recipe called "New Burton Ale". He also brewed a London XXXX Ale from soft water, according to the Burton recipe but mashing at 65 and 88°C.

c) NEW BURTON ALE. 1860.

Ingredients:

Malt	2.5 kg. pale.
Water	4 ltr. soft per mash.
Adjuncts	pinch of calcium sulphate
Hops	225 g. Kentish such as Goldings.
Sugar	none.
Yeast	30 g. top fermenter.

Conditions:

Mash temperature	78°C.
Mash time	2 hours.

The wort is drained off and then the draff mashed for a second time.

Mash temperature	83°C.
Mash time	1 hour.
Sparge volume	8 ltr.
Hop boiling time	2 hours
Initial gravity	not recorded.
Storage time	6 weeks.
Expected volume	not recorded.
Alcohol content	6%

d)   OXFORD OLD ALE. 1880.

Ingredients:

Malt	2.5 kg. pale
Hops	85 g. Hallertauer or Goldings.
Water	4 ltr. soft per mash.
Sugar	1 kg.
Yeast	30 g. top fermenter.

Conditions:

Mash temperature	75°C.
Mash time	2 hours.
2nd mash.	
Mash temperature	85°C.
Mash time	90 minutes.
Sparge volume	10 ltr.
Hop boiling time	90 minutes.
Initial gravity	1.028 g/cm^3.
Fermentation temperature	15°C.
Bottling gravity	1.010 g/cm^3.
Storage time	2 weeks.
Expected volume	25-39 ltr.
Alcohol content	3.5%.

e)   WORKER'S ALE. 1798.

Ingredients:

Malt	2.5 kg. pale, amber, or brown.
Water	To suit the malt.
Adjuncts	chillies.
	coriander
	salt
Hops	40 g. Kentish.
Sugar	50 g.
Yeast	30 g top fermenter.

Conditions:

Mash temperature	85°C.
Mash time	2-3 hours.
Sparge volume	10 ltr.
Hop boiling time	1.5 hours.
Initial gravity	1.025 g/cm^3.
Fermentation temperature	20°C.
Bottling gravity	1.012 g/cm^3.
Storage time	3-6 months.
Expected volume	25-30 ltr.
Alcohol content	3.5%.

The bottling gravity is at the upper limit for safety. Perhaps oak barrels were much stronger than screw top bottles are today.

f) DORSET OLD ALE. 1880.

Ingredients:

Malt	2.5 kg. pale.
Water	5 ltr. soft per mash.
Adjuncts	none.
Hops	130 g. Kentish.
Sugar	none.
Yeast	30 g. top fermenter.

Conditions:

Mash temperature	75°C.
Mash time	2 hours.
2nd mash	
Temperature	88°C.
Time	1 hour.
Sparge volume	10 ltr.
Hop boiling time	90 minutes.
Initial gravity	1.065 g/cm^3.
Fermentation temperature	15°C.
Bottling gravity	1.013 g/cm^3.
Storage time	2-6 months.
Expected volume	15-20 ltr.
Alcohol content	7.5%

The bottling gravity is high.

g) MILD ALE. 1821.

Nowadays brewers use crystal malt, black malt, roasted barley or torrified barley. Traditionally they were brewed only with pale malt. The storage time was very short and the addition of dark malt covers the cloudiness and so mild ale fell victim to the clear beer brigade.

Ingredients:

Malt	3.5 kg. pale or amber.
Water	4 ltr. soft per mash.
Adjuncts	none.
Hops	145 g. Northern Brewer.
Sugar	None.
Yeast	30 g. top fermenter.

Conditions:

The cracked malt was left two days in the air to prove.

Mash temperature	71°C.
Mash time	2 hours.

2nd mash
Temperature .... 76°C.
Time .... 2.5 hours.
Sparge volume .... 10 ltr.
Hop boiling time .... 30 minutes.
The two worts were kept separate until fermentation.
Initial gravity .... 1.045 g/cm³.
Fermentation temperature .... 22°C.
Yeast added at 26°C as the worts cool.
Bottling gravity............... Fermented out.
Storage time .... 2-4 weeks.
Expected volume .... 20-25 ltr.
Alcohol content............... 6%.

The same author brews a brown ale using the same recipe, but adding 300 g. black malt.

h) SCOTCH X ALE. 1821.

Ingredients:

Malt........................... 2.5 kg. white.
                    60 g. black.
Water.......................... 4 ltr. soft per mash.
Adjuncts .... none.
Hops .... 50 g. Kentish.
Sugar.......................... none
Yeast .... 30 g. top fermenter.

Conditions:

Mash temperature............. 72°C.
Mash time..................... 90 minutes.
2nd mash
Mash temperature............. 83°C.
Mash time..................... 60 minutes.
Sparge volume .... 8 ltr.
Hop boiling time .... 90 minutes.
Initial gravity .... 1.025 g/cm³.
Fermentation temperature .... not recorded
Bottling gravity............... 1.001 g/cm³.
Storage time .... 2 weeks
Expected volume .... 30 ltr.
Alcohol content............... 3.5%

A Scottish XXX Ale of 1880 was mashed with pale malt, 3°C hotter, fermented out at 15°C from an initial gravity of 1.040 and stored for 6 weeks.

i) EAST INDIA PALE ALE. 1862.

Ingredients:

Malt	3.0 kg. white.
Water	4 ltr. per mash hard Burton water and well boiled to remove hydrogen carbonate hardness.
Adjuncts	Calcium carbonate.
Hops	270 g. Kentish.
Sugar	none.
Yeast	30 g. top fermenter.

Conditions:

Mash temperature	74°C.
Mash time	2 hours.
2nd mash	
Temperature	82°C.
Time	1 hour.
Sparge volume	8 ltr.
Hop boiling time	1.5 hours.
Initial gravity	1.024 g/cm^3.
Fermentation temperature	not recorded but fermented out in 2 days.
Bottling gravity	1.010 g/cm^3.
Storage time	4 weeks.
Expected volume	30 ltr.
Alcohol content	3.5%.

A variation of this brew was a London Old Ale, which was mashed twice to give an initial gravity of 1.041 and stored for 6 months.

j) BROWN ALE or TWOPENNY ALE. 1821.

Ingredients:

Malt	2 gallons amber or brown.
Water	3.5 gallons soft for each mash.
Adjuncts	none
Hops	0.25 lbs/mash.
Sugar	none.
Yeast	top fermenter.

Conditions:

Mash temperature	70°C.
Mash time	1.5 hours.

2nd mash
Temperature....................70°C.
Time ....1.5 hours.
Hop boiling time ....1 hour for each mash which is boiled separately and then mixed in the fermentation vat.
Initial gravity ....not recorded but probably 1.020 g/cm^3.
Fermentation temperature ....fast.
Bottling gravity................flat
Storage time ....less than 2 weeks.
Expected volume...............not recorded.
Alcohol content................not recorded.

k)   STRONG or OCTOBER ALE. 1821.

Ingredients:

Malt.............................3 kg. pale.
Water...........................no volume recorded, but soft.
Adjuncts ....pinch table salt and the same of flour.
Hops ....100 g/wort.
Sugar...........................none.
Yeast...........................300 g. (probably a liquid slurry from another brew).

Conditions:

Mash temperature..............74°C.
Mash time......................1.75 hours.
2nd mash
Temperature....................79°C.
Time ....2 hours.
Sparge volume.................not recorded.
Hop boiling time ....30 minutes.
Initial gravity ....not recorded but probably 1.055 g/cm^3.
Fermentation temperature ....17°C.
Bottling gravity................flat.
Storage time ....long. (12 weeks?)
Expected volume...............not recorded.
Alcohol content................7%.

The following recipes come from an undated Yorkshire cookery book. The authoress remains also anonymous, being simply described as an "Experienced Cook." I would guess it to be late eighteenth century. I have prepared the recipes somewhat for the modern kitchen as most of them start with sentences such as, "Pour forty two gallons of hot water, not quite boiling on eight bushels of malt..."

l)   WELSH ALE. 18th century.

Ingredients:

Malt	3.2 kg. pale.
Water	4-6 ltr.
Adjuncts	none
Hops	20 g. (perhaps a misprint.)
Sugar	none
Yeast	top fermenter

Conditions:

Mash temperature	nearly boiling poured onto the malt.
Mash time	3 hours.
Sparge	wort run onto the hops and the draff remashed for a small beer.
Hop boiling time	Infused in hot water for an unspecified time, then boiled with the unsparged wort. The infusion was used for a small beer.
Initial gravity	not recorded but probably strong.
Fermentation temperature	22°C.
Bottling gravity	flat
Storage time	6 weeks
Expected volume	not recorded.
Alcohol content	not recorded.

It appears that the draff was remashed for a table beer and the hops too were used a second time for this weaker beer. The same cook describes the difference, as far as she was concerned between beer, ale and small beer. They are all brewed according to the same recipe, but a beer takes just under twice the malt quantity of an ale. Hence for beer the above recipe would read the same quantities except she used 5.6 kg. malt (and a little more mash water). Beer received 60 g., ale 20-40 g. and table or small beer the second hand hops from the ale or beer brew. Hops may have been hard to come by in the North of England and hence these thrifty brews.

m)   TABLE BEER. 18th century.

Ingredients:

Malt	2.7 kg. pale.
Water	2 ltr./mash.
Adjuncts	none
Hops	15 gm.
Sugar	none
Yeast	top fermenter.

Method:

Pour 3 ltr. of warm water on the malt and stand for 30 mins. Warm to 70°C and mash for 2½ hours.

Run the wort off, then add 3 ltr. of water at 70°C. Mash for 30 minutes and then drain the second wort off.

Mash one more time with the remaining water for 1 hour.

Mix all the worts and add the hops after infusing them.

Boil the worts and hops for 1 hour.

Ferment quickly and drink after 3-4 weeks.

Beer was normally brewed in March because thundery or warm weather sends it sour. Our cook tells that a teaspoon of salt or wormwood per jug of ale, will rectify this. Ramming a linen bag of dried hops into the bung hole was a prophylactic cure for this ill. The above recipe is maybe unique, for it is the only evidence I have found in the English language, which uses a type of continental decoction process. The temperatures I have reconstructed on the basis that water one "can just bear" is around 60-70°C.

n)   WINDSOR ALE. 18th century.

Ingredients:

Malt.............................3.6 kg. pale.
Water...........................not specified.
Adjuncts ....2.5 g. coriander.
                               2.5 g. seeds of paradise (peppercorn).
                               2.5 g. orange peel.
                               25 g. ground liquorice root.
Hops ....180 g. soaked 12 hours in cold water.
Sugar...........................40 g. honey

Method:

One third of the above are mashed at 82°C for 75 minutes, stood an hour and then boiled one hour.

The second third are mashed at 90°C for 45 minutes, and then boiled for three hours.

The final portion are mashed at 70°C for 45 minutes and then stood for the same length.

All three worts are sparged, mixed and fermented.

When fermentation has ceased the following are beaten in:
        Hops.
        Pinch of salt.
        Handful flour.
        Pinch of ground ginger.
        Pinch of ground caraway seeds.
The recipe then continues with a dissertation on the illegality of using the above "drugs" excepting in private houses, under a penalty of £200 and forfeiture of all utensils. Drugists who sold to brewers were liable to be fined £500. There is no further information on the beer itself!

o) ALE ON A SMALL SCALE. 18th century.

The British seem to have made ale rather as we nowadays make tea. This next beer must be the ultimate in "quick brew".

"Put a handful of malt, into a tea kettle , and fill it with water, rather under boiling heat: when it has stood some time, pour it off and fill it up again, but with boiling water. Continue pouring it off and filling it up again until the malt is tasteless, then boil the liquor with a few hops in it, and when lukewarm add a little yeast, to ferment it. One pint of malt, and four ounces of hops will produce ten quarts of ale much better than porter."

Whose porter? Assuming a very good mash, this ale would be at best be described as "thin". But as ale was served for breakfast to David Copperfield, 2.5% was probably plenty strong enough prior to a day's work. This recipe certainly has all the trade marks of a school kitchen. It may be useful though as a quick and easy brew to test hops of unknown quality.

p) OAT ALE. 1770.

Another of Watkin's great little recipes. The oat malt is prepared in the same way as barley malt and gently kilned. Only the very best oats are of use. If you want to save yourself the trouble of making oat malt, then buy some oat flakes from the health food shop and mix them with about 20% by weight of barley malt to supply the diastase. It is worth boiling the oat flakes before starting to mash in order to soften up the heavy proteins.

i)   3 kg. oat malt is cracked and left two days without cover, in a cool place, to prove.

ii)   Pour 9 ltr. of cold hard water over the malt, and leave it to stand 13 hours at room temperature.

iii)   Run the wort off and strain it slowly through a linen bag containing 40 g. hops.

iv)   Ferment the wort out inside 2 days and fill into bottles.

v)   The beer should be drunk within two months.

There are problems with wild yeast fermentations. As the wort is never boiled, the mash must be really quite cold or fermentation will commence before the mash is finished. I have found the 13 hour wait problematic as fermentation can set in during this time and I have had to discard the wort.

In any case its worth boiling the wort with the hops in order to extract the flavour.

Oat ale can also be made using any of the recipes for barley brews. Many writers lament the passing of oat beverages. The low mash temperature reflects the high content of heavy protein molecules to be found in oats. Oat beers should lend themselves to recipe (m), or any of the German recipes which include a special protein mash for sticky malts.

q)   PORTER FOR HARD WATER. 1880.

Ingredients:

> Malt..............................3.0 kg. pale.
> 400 g. amber or brown.
> 250 g. black.
> Water............................4 ltr. hard.
> Adjuncts ....none.
> Hops ....125 g. Sussex.
> Sugar.............................1 kg.
> Yeast ....30 g. top fermenter.

Conditions:

> Mash temperature..............67°C.
> Mash time.......................2 hours.
> 2nd mash
> Mash temperature..............80°C.
> Mash time.......................1 hour.
> Sparge volume..................10 ltr.
> Hop boiling time ....1.5 hours.
> Initial gravity ....1.021 g/cm^3.
> Fermentation temperature....Fermented out in 2 days.
> Bottling gravity.................flat.
> Storage time ....3-4 weeks.
> Expected volume...............25 ltr.
> Alcohol content................3%

r)   "PORTER, CHEAP and GOOD." 18th century.

   "Linseed, 1 oz.; the same of Spanish juice and ginger; hops 1½ oz.; malt 1 lb.; liquorice, ½ oz.; sugar and treacle each, 1½ lbs. Boil with 4½ gallons of water, down to 3.5 gallons; also add a little Pearl or Iceland Moss. When cool, stir yeast into it, and let it ferment."

   This must be one of the quaintest beer recipes yet and certainly worth a try. Spanish juice is actually liquorice and it is not clear what the 18th century distinction was. Iceland Moss is not a moss but a lichen. (*Cetraria Islandica*). It looks nothing like a moss, is usually brown in colour and can be found throughout the North on heather moors.

s)   PORTER. 1798.

Ingredients:

> Malt..............................4 kg. amber.
> Water............................4 ltr. to suit the malt.
> Adjuncts ....250 g. liquorice.

Prior to casking were also added:

	120 g. chillies.
	4 g. ginger root.
	1 red pepper.
Hops	120 g. Goldings.
Sugar	250 g. black treacle.
Yeast	30 g. top fermenter.

Conditions:

Mash temperature	82°C.
Mash time	2-3 hours.
Sparge volume	12 ltr.
Hop boiling time	2 hours with the other adjuncts.
Initial gravity	1.045 g/cm³.
Fermentation temperature	fast.
Bottling gravity	flat.
Storage time	2-3 weeks.
Expected volume	25 ltr.
Alcohol content	6%.

Stouts.

The term "stout" is difficult to define. Some are among the strongest and bitterest beers available and other are very gentle on the palate. The milk stouts, which contain non-fermentable lactose, are slightly sweet. Others on the Continent are brewed from crystal malt alone, which also provides little fermentable extract and thus produces a nutritional but nearly non-alcoholic brew. The addition of lactose, caramel and other non-fermentables is not mentioned in historical recipes but a very good milk stout for feeding mothers may contain between 15-30 g/ltr. beer of lactose. The caramel colour can be obtained by heating household sugar and a little water with constant stirring, until the desired colour and taste are achieved. This can then be used as an adjunct to, or surrogate for crystal malt. One such a beer is sold commercially in Germany as *Karamalz*, and is highly thought of for convalescents and feeding mothers.

The best known stout is of course Guinness, which some believe is made from pale malt and roasted barley. Its bitter qualities wouldn't be from the hops alone, produced by a delicate balance between the hops and burnt barley.

I'm not going to pretend that I can tell you how to make Guinness, but the following stouts should satisfy.

t) A DUBLIN STOUT by Mr. Guinness. 1865.

Ingredients:

Malt	2.9 kg. pale.
	125 g. black.
Water	5 l/mash soft.
Adjuncts	none
Hops	290 g. Kentish.
Sugar	none.
Yeast	30 g. top fermenter.

Conditions:

Mash temperature	75°C.
Mash time	75 minutes.
2nd mash.	
Temperature	83°C.
Time	45 minutes.
Sparge volume	10 ltr.
Hop boiling time	1.5 hours.
Initial gravity	1.033 g/cm^3.
Fermentation temperature	21-26°C.
Fermentation time	4 days.
Bottling gravity	1.009 g/cm^3.
Storage time	4-6 weeks.
Expected volume	26 l.
Alcohol content	4.5%.

This brew was carried out in London by a Mr. Guinness of Dublin and recorded by Amsinck, who was rather scathing about the practice of double mashing. There is no doubt though, that mashing twice is an excellent method of gaining the maximum extract from malt in rather less than perfect domestic kitchen breweries.

u) DOUBLE STOUT. 1880.

Ingredients:

Malt	2.6 kg. pale.
	140 g. black.
	750 g. amber or dark.
Water	5 ltr/mash soft.
Adjuncts	none.
Hops	120 g. Kentish.
Sugar	none.
Yeast	30 g. top fermenter.

Conditions:

Mash temperature	70°C.
Mash time	2 hours.
2nd mash.	
Mash temperature	80°C.
Mash time	30 minutes.
Sparge volume	6 ltr.
Hop boiling time	1.5 hours.
Initial gravity	1.029 g/cm³.
Fermentation temperature	18-22°C.
Fermentation time	2 days.
Bottling gravity	1.014 g/cm³.
Storage time	not recorded.
Expected volume	26 ltr.
Alcohol content	4%.

The bottling gravity is rather high. It is also noteworthy that beers containing so much dark malt should be brewed using soft water, but this was typical for Irish Stouts. Gentler hop quantities are also more usual.

v) TREBLE STOUT. 1885.

Ingredients:

Malt	3.8 kg. pale.
	700 g. amber or brown
	150 g. black.
Water	4 ltr. per mash soft.
Adjuncts	none.
Hops	180 g. Yellow East or Mid Kent.
Sugar	none.
Yeast	30 g. top fermenter.

Conditions:

             Mash temperature.............72°C.
             Mash time.....................90 minutes.
             2nd mash
             Mash temperature.............79°C.
             Mash time.....................1 hour.
             Sparge volume.................10 ltr.
             Hop boiling time..............3 hours. The hops were probably added a
                                          little at a time during the boiling.
             Initial gravity.................1.035 g/cm³.
             Fermentation temperature....not recorded.
             Fermentation time............3 days.
             Bottling gravity................1.010 g/cm³.
             Storage time...................not recorded.
             Expected volume..............30 ltr.
             Alcohol content................4.7%.

The next stout made in this particular brewery used slightly different conditions, not by design but simply because different malt was available and the mash settled at a different temperature. This element of surprise is what the house-brewer can most look forward to, and that which he rarely finds in the pub keg. Here is the new set of conditions as recorded by the brewmaster.

w)   TREBLE STOUT II.

Ingredients:

             Malt............................3.7 kg. pale.
                                          1.1 kg. amber or brown.
                                          150 g. black.
             Hops...........................160 g. Yellow East or Mid Kent.

Conditions:

             Mash temperature.............71°C.
             Mash time.....................2 hours.
             2nd mash.
             Mash temperature.............79°C.
             Mash time.....................1.5 hours.
             Initial gravity.................1.034 g/cm³.
             Fermentation temperature....not recorded.
             Fermentation time............2 days.
             Expected volume..............33 ltr.
             Alcohol content................4.7%.

x)   VERY STRONG ALE. 18th Century by Otto.

This recipe for an English Ale is recorded in an early 19th century German publication and purports to explain how the English brewed very strong beers. It stands in stark contrast to the thrifty "cook book" recipes from the same period. One wonders if there is more admiration from Herrn Otto for the expensive method than accuracy. This recipe no doubt existed but if it was really English is a good question.

Ingredients:

Malt	1 kg. air dried wheat malt.
	1 kg. air dried barley malt.
	1 kg. pale malt.
Water	6 ltr/mash soft.
Adjuncts	none.
Hops	150 g. Kentish.
Sugar	none.
Yeast	30 g. top fermenter.

Conditions:

Mash temperature	71°C.
Mash time	2 hours.
2nd mash.	
Temperature	79°C.
Time	1.5 hours.
Sparge volume	12 ltr.
Hop boiling time	5-8 hours.

The wort after boiling should contain about 30% soluble protein and maltose. Wort containing so much gluten (from the gluten rich air dried malts,) was, according to the writer, able to provide the environment and nutrient required by the yeast, to be able to work in alcohol concentrations of about 10%.

This concentrated wort was cooled to about 7-16°C, diluted to an initial gravity of 1.075 g/cm^3, and fermented in vats with a large surface area exposed to the air.

After the initial fermentation was finished, the young beer was kegged and stored at less than 15°C for 9-12 months, during which time the alcohol concentration rises to 10% and much of the proteins precipitate out. The Germans apparently admired such beers greatly, for this style of fermentation seems to produce a very pure product.

Otto says that porter was made in much the same way, stronger hopped and given a fine bitterness by the addition of minute amounts of strychnine! If there is a limit to our quest for authentic and original beers we must have just reached it!

y) MUM-ALE.

This beer is reputed to have originated in Braunschweig (Brunswick) and is mentioned by Pepys in 1644 as having been popular in London. Everyone seems to have had a guess at the origin of the name "Mum", so why shouldn't I have my twopenneth. Favourite is that the brewmaster Christoph Mumme first brewed this beer in Braunschweig in 1492. The Oxford Dictionary recalls an anonymous quote of 1640 "I thinke your're drunk with Lubecks beere or Brunswick's Mum." However the German phrase "keinen Mumm in den Knochen haben", can be translated as "knackered or gutless". The opposite then "Mumm haben", implies strength and energy, precisely what this beer will give you. This recipe is certainly among the oldest in this book, uses a grout and is a wheat and oat ale.

To make five gallons.

Ingredients:

Malt	4-5 pints wheat malt.
	4-5 pints oat malt.
	4-5 pints beans.
Water	3-4 gallons soft for mashing and sparging.
Adjuncts	4 oz. of the inner rind of the fir. 2 oz. of fir and birch tops. ¼ handful of Rosa Solis made from burnet, betony, marjoram, avens, penny royal, elder flowers, and thyme, not to forget the same amount of Cardus Benedictus, a pinch of cardamom and bayberries.

Conditions:

Mash temperature	"according to the art".
Mash time	"until it begins to work".
Sparging	It is not absolutely clear if the mash was sparged or not. I suspect it was, then left to ferment out. It was definitely, "casked with an unbroken egg and not tapped for two years". Had no body the courage? "A sea voyage," it was reported, "greatly improved the beer!" Was this the first "Export Beer"?

No wonder Pope wrote:

> *"The clamorous crowd is hush'd with mugs of mum,*
> *Till all, turned equal, send a general hum."*

We owe this recipe to a Victorian collector of strange brews, a Mr. Bickerdyke.

z)   RINGWOOD ALE. 18th century.

To finish off, here is an unexpurgated version which I haven't worked up for the modern kitchen. Let this be your prentice brew.
Answers please in a bottle to the author!

"This brewing produces two barrels and a half from the quarter. The best pale malt and pocket hops are used, at the rate of 6 pounds to the quarter. Turn on the first mash at 180°, and the second at 190°. Pitch the tun at 60° and cleanse at 80°. Mash successively one hour and three quarters of an hour, standing an hour and a half, and two hours. Add in the tun two pounds of yeast for every barrel, and coat with salt and flour after the first scimming."

German Recipes.

German recipes are much more complicated than the English. They rely not on esoteric ingredients for their variety but more on the wide ranges of mash temperatures during the warming of the mash, to provide nuances in their brews. Also the bottom fermenting yeasts work at lower temperatures which in itself leads to a purer fermentation process with fewer by-products being produced. As with the English beers, the type of hops used and the production of the malt is decisive.

Although the recipes differ little from the basic recipe, the nuances are so subtle that each recipe requires careful description and should be followed exactly. Always take care to produce thick porridge-like mashes and when heating them see that they don't burn to the bottom of the pan.

a)   BASIC RECIPE FOR A PILSNER.

Ingredients:

                Malt........................3 kg. Bohemian.
                Water.......................5 ltr. soft.
                Hops ....100 g. Saaz.
                Yeast ....20 g. bottom fermenter.
                Sugar.......................1 kg. (optional).

Method:

   i)   Grind the malt.

   ii)   Mix the malt with 3l water at 40°C and regulate mash to give a thick porridge at 35°C.

   iii)   Check that the pH is 5.0-5.5.

   iv)   Mark the volume of the mash on the outside of the mash bucket with an indelible felt pen. Make another mark at ⅔ the volume.

v) Ladle ⅓ of the mash into a saucepan of at least 3 ltr. capacity. (Don't use aluminium pots.) Cover and insulate the main mash.

vi) Warm the saucepan slowly until 70°C. Care and stirring are essential to prevent hot spots and burning. Add a little more water if you are worried.

vii) When the saucepan contents are at around 65-70°C, turn off the plate, insulate the pot and stand for 30 minutes.

viii) After this time, check the temperature of the bucket and bring it back to 35°C.
Use as little water as possible.

ix) Bring the contents of the saucepan to boiling point as quickly as possible and mix it with the main mash in the bucket. After stirring to eliminate hot spots, the temperature should settle out at around 50-55°C.

x) Ladle off 1/3 of the mash into the saucepan and bring it slowly, over about 30 minutes, to the boil.

xi) Mix the two mashes and stir. The temperature should rise to about 65°C.

xii) Place the mash bucket in the waterbath (12) and hold the mash temperature at 65°C for 2 hours. The temperature should be frequently checked and regulated.

xiii) If the quick mash method (*Kurzmaischverfahren*) is being used, the mash should now be terminated. Otherwise after 2 hours, ⅓ of the mash is again removed, brought to the boil and re-mixed with the main mash. This should bring the temperature to 75°C. This temperature is then maintained for 15-30 minutes before the mash process is finally ended.

xiv) The wort is run off, and the draff sparged as for the infusion method. Boil the wort with the hops and prepare it for fermentation by adjusting the starting gravity to 1.035 g/cm^3.

xv) Add a good working bottom fermenting yeast to the wort and cover the fermentation vat. The temperature for fermentation should be kept at 7-10°C.

xvi) Check that fermentation has actually commenced. If it hasn't, add a new yeast sample. Placing the fermentation vat in a warmer ambience should remain a last resort. The density of the wort will drop to about 1.010g/cm^3 during the next 8-10 days.

xvii) Remove any hop resins and unhealthy looking yeast foam which may appear during the fermentation and keg the beer as soon as it has reached the finishing gravity.

xviii) Store the beer at about 2-8°C for at least 6-8 weeks. If it is not clear or doesn't taste right after this time, leave it another 2-4 weeks.

xix) Serve the beer at its storage temperature.

b) AUGSBURGER BREW reported by August Ernst Müller. 1845.

This method by Müller is exceptionally complicated, but very interesting. It seems that brewers of Müller's acquaintance had similar problems to those which exercise the modern house-brewer, for it contains special features designed to take care of poorly germinated malt containing too much protein, as well as malt which has been ground too fine with the consequent aggravation caused by the presence of fine flour. The recipe given here is in a much shortened form. The original by Müller required seven sides!

A 10 ltr. bucket with a tap for running the wort off is required (12). The bucket should also have a false wire mesh bottom, above the level of the tap, to prevent the draff blocking the tap.

Ingredients:

Malt.....................1.4 kg. dark, kilned at 150°C for 3 hours.
1.2 kg. Bohemian, kilned at 70°C for 2 hours.
Water.....................6 ltr. moderate to hard.
Hops ....159 g. Hallertauer.
Sugar.....................1 kg. (optional).
Yeast ....30 g. top fermenter.

Method:

i)   Grind the malt.

ii)   Mix the malt into 4 ltr. water and rest the malt for 2 hours at 30°C.

iii)   Draw 1.5 ltr. off through the tap, stirring all the while so that as much as possible of the fine malt powder is run off too. The drawn off liquid is called the "cold portion" and is kept in a pot to one side.

iv)   Hot water at 85°C is added to the mash until with stirring a mash temperature of 47-57°C is reached.

v)   Open the tap immediately and during the next half hour run off the so called "warm portion". This should be clear and the mash must not be stirred during the run off.

vi)   While the warm portion is running off, dilute the cold portion with 1 ltr. water and bring to the boil. This coagulates the fine powder and should help the beer clear and make sparging easier. Boil until the coagulation is observed to take place.

vii)   Pour the cold portion, which is now boiling, back into the mash tun, stir it well and leave it to mash for 2 hours.

viii)   Bring the warm portion up to 57°C and maintain this temperature.

ix)   Boil the mash, with frequent stirring, for 1-2 hours. As the farinaceous malt substance has been coagulated, the risk of burning has been reduced. Take care though. This long boiling process should help break down any heavy proteins which may prevent enzyme access to the starch. If there is no reason to suspect a malt of poor quality, the time may be shortened.

x)   Mix the boiling mash into the warm portion so that the temperature of the warm portion never exceeds 65°C. The enzymes in the mash have been destroyed by the boiling, but not those in the warm portion. These are still needed to further the mash and convert the freed starch to sugar.

xi) Mash for 1 hour at 65°C.

xii) Draw off the wort, sparge and work up the beer as described in the basic Pilsner recipe. The wort is cooked for 1½ hours with the hops. Müller doesn't indicate the strength of this beer but about 4.5% would probably be about right.

c)   HALLER DOUBLE BEER according to an old Bavarian method recorded in 1845.

Ingredients:

Malt	2.5 kg. dark, kilned at 120°C for 3 hours. 200 g. black malt.
Water	6 ltr. as it comes from the tap but reduce the hops if temporary hard.
Hops	200 g. Hallertauer.
Sugar	1 kg. optional.
Yeast	30 g. top fermenter.

Method:

i)   Grind the malt and after mixing it with 3 ltr. water, let it stand 2-3 hours at room temperature.

ii)   Boil 2.5 ltr. water and stir in 0.5 ltr. aliquots until the mash temperature reaches about 40°C.

iii) First thick mash.
      The thick part of the mash, which is at the bottom of the mash tun, is ladled out into a saucepan, leaving only the thin liquid in the tun. The porridge is slowly brought to the boil and then gently boiled for 45-90 minutes.

iv)   The boiling porridge is returned to the mash tun and the temperature, which should reach about 50°C, is maintained for about 15 minutes.

v)   Second thick mash.
      The process described in (iii) and (iv) is repeated. The mash temperature should rise to around 60°C.

vi)   The thin clarifying mash.
      Allow the thick mash substance to settle out and then ladle off the thin liquid into a saucepan. Bring this to the boil and re-mix it with the mash. The temperature should now rise to 65°C.

vii) Recover the wort and sparge the draff in the normal way.

viii) Boil the wort for 1-2 hours with the hops, strain and dilute the wort to a density of $1.070g/cm^3$.

ix)   Ferment out at 17-20°C with a top fermenting yeast, keg and store for 2-3 months. The alcohol content will be about 8.5%.

121

d)   BAVARIAN BROWN BEER. Recorded 1842.

Ingredients:

Malt.............................2.5 kg. Bohemian.
                              250 g. black.
Water...........................6 ltr. moderately hard.
Hops ....70 g. Hallertauer.
Sugar...........................1 kg. optional.
Yeast ....30 g. bottom fermenter.

Method:

A mash tun with a run-off tap is required (12).

i)   The ground malt is mixed with enough cold water to make a thick porridge and this is kept at 15°C for 5 hours.

ii)   Boiling water is run in with stirring until the temperature of the mash reaches 36-40°C.

iii)   Mark how full the mash tun is and ⅔ of this height with an indelible felt tip pen.

iv)   Ladle out ⅓ of the thick mash substance into a saucepan and heat this at 90°C for 30 minutes. Take care that it doesn't burn.

v)   Mix the thick mash with the main mash, which should bring the temperature to about 52°C. Maintain this temperature for 15 minutes.

vi)   Repeat (iv) and (v) but this time maintain the final temperature (approx 63°C) for 30 minutes.

vii)   During this last half hour halt, repeat (iv) and (v) one more time. This should bring the mash temperature up to 70-72°C. Insulate the tun and maintain this temperature for 2-3 hours.

viii) The wort is now run out the bottom of the tun and poured back into the top until it begins to run out clear. Run all the wort off and then sparge as normal. Make sure that the fine powder which should now be on top of the draff, is not stirred into the body of the malt, where it can cause blockages in the sparging.

ix)   Boil the wort for 1 hour with the hops.

x)   Work the beer up as described in the basic recipe, aiming at an initial gravity of 1.020 g/cm³ at 12°C. Ferment at this temperature with bottom fermenting yeast. The yeast should sink after about 6-8 days and as soon as it is fermented out (flat) the beer may be kegged. It will need storing for about 6-10 weeks and should contain about 2.5% alcohol.

e)   PILS.

To obtain a fine light Pils, the Bavarian Brown Beer recipe (d) can be used with only pale Bohemian malt, very soft water and Saaz hops. An initial gravity of 1.025 g/cm³ will give a beer with about 3.5% alcohol content.

f) COMMON BEER from the Tyrol, reconstructed from an 18th century description.

The Bavarian brown beer method should be used.

Ingredients:

Malt	4 kg. Viennese
Water	7 ltr. moderately hard.
Hops	80 g. Hallertauer.
Sugar	1 kg. (optional).
Yeast	30 g. top fermenter.

Conditions:

Initial gravity	1.045 g/cm^3.
Fermentation temperature	17°C.
Fermentation time	2-7 days.
Bottling gravity	1.010 g/cm^3.
Storage time	6-12 weeks.

g) MARCH BEER from the Tyrol, reconstructed from an 18th century description.

The method probably used was very close to that described for a Bavarian Brown Beer (e).

Ingredients:

Malt	4 kg. Bohemian.
Water	6 ltr. soft.
Hops	160 g. Hallertauer.
Sugar	1 kg. (optional).
Yeast	30 g. top fermenter.

Conditions:

Initial gravity	1.045 g/cm^3.
Fermentation temperature	18°C.
Bottling gravity	1.012 g/cm^3.
Storage time	6-12 weeks.

h) FRANKEN BIER. 1845.

This method was described by Müller but mainly so that he could point out and complain about the sin and error of brewers in Franconia. The recipe does produce a thinner beer, more rich in alcohol.

i) Put the crushed malt into a mash tub with a tap and wire sieve bottom (12) and make a thick porridge with water between 25-78°C. This haphazard temperature description leaves much to the brewers discretion but no apology was made for this!

ii) After a short time run this weak wort off to leave a liquid depth of 3 inches in the tub.

iii) Bring the weak wort to the boil, then allow it to cool to 90°C before adding it again to the mash tub.

iv) The temperature in the mash tub should settle after stirring at around 72-84°C. Leave the mash for 90 minutes after which time the temperature should fall to around 55-60°C.

v) During this mash time, remove an amount of the wort, heat it to about 85°C and add the hops. Maintain the temperature at around 85°C.

vi) Remove the hops with a sieve, join the two worts and wash the draff, work up and ferment with a top fermenting yeast in the normal way.

i) COVENT BIER. 18th century.

Covent is the old form of Convent, which can still be found in names such as Covent Garden. Hence this beer must have its origins in monastic life. It is reported by Müller, and the main feature of a Covent Bier is that after twice mashing the malt and then sparging, the draff was soaked in a quarter of the amount of cold water again in order to make a second beer form the draff. This soaking proceeds until the main wort from that draff has been boiled with the hops. The cold wort is then run off the draff, brought to the boil and then run back onto the draff. One thus achieves a so called "Covent extract", which, when run off, is again brought to the boil and then run through the hops which were also used for the main brew.

If this beer was brewed in a monastery, it certainly wasn't for Benedictine monks who were famed for the strength of their brews. This was a poor man's drink more appropriate to the so called "Bettelorden", such as the Franciscan or Dominican Orders.

It was also fermented with a bottom fermenting yeast, which was unusual before the 19th century and only monks had the skill and knowledge of these yeasts. The only advantages of such a brew are that it really only costs the electricity to boil a few litres of water and is a refreshing, if thin beer, which may be enjoyed at any time without fear of becoming affected by the alcohol or hops. It should not be compared in taste to normal beers and is probably really only worth trying if one suspects that a mash or sparge have been inefficient or some doubtful hops are to be tested.

j) FARRENBACHER WEIßBIER. Recorded in the 19th century.

This beer is of special interest as it was brewed at the Farrenbacher Gut, a manor house near Nürnberg. The recipe was kept a house secret and a certain Herr Müller seems to have contrived through some form of brewers espionage to steal the method. Despite his efforts I had to reconstruct the recipe as someone had removed some vital pages from the library edition I obtained. Farrenbacher revenge? It serves to demonstrate what an incredible variety of beers must have once been available and how jealously their secrets were guarded. The recipe is by German standards very simple, not to say primitive. I believe it to date from the Middle Ages.

i)   Very pale barley malt (2.5 kg.) is mashed (some say in mineral water, others in very soft spring water), as described in recipe (h) but stop after instruction (iv). Use plenty of water for the mash, so that a fairly thin consistency is obtained.

ii) Sparge as normal.

iii) In order to keep as much protein in the wort as possible, the hot and cold breaks are omitted. The wort is boiled for only 8 minutes with 20 g. hops. The hop taste can thus be hardly detected and virtually no proteins are able to coagulate and precipitate out. By the same token few will be able to dissolve in the wort.

iv) Dilute the wort to give a starting gravity of 1.040 g/cm^3.

v)   Ferment out with a top fermenting yeast at 11°C.

vi) Store for 6 weeks.

This should be a beer low in dextrines but high in nourishment. All the sugar available is converted into alcohol, which gives the beer a feeling of a good if cloudy wine. Because of the slight hop taste, such beer was often additionally flavoured with herbs such as woodruff (see chapter 10. on hop surrogates).

k) BOCKBIER or SALVATORBIER. 18th century.

This is a South German Lent beer which contains much nutritional protein to counteract the effect of the fast. One is allowed to drink as much as one likes in Lent! The beers may be made from light or moderately dark malts, depending on the water available and the taste of the drinker. They should be brewed according to the Bavarian Brown Beer method (d) but the trick is to boil the wort for 3-5 hours, thus causing the coagulated protein to redissolve in the wort instead of precipitating out. This is similar to Otto's English method for making very rich porters and ales.

The boiled wort has a density of around 1.070 g/cm^3. This is cooled quickly to about 8°C and diluted to a starting gravity of 1.030 g/cm^3.

A bottom fermenting yeast is added and the main fermentation completed in around 14 days. The secondary fermentation in the bottles or keg lasts several months.

l)   GRUEL BEER from Schleswig-Holstein. (17th century.)

This North German beer is another economy drink which has only the speed with which it is ready to drink to recommend it. It is reported by Adolf Baum in his book about Schleswig specialities.

A bag is filled with 10l of wheat bran and a few handfuls of rye flour. The whole is dampened. A smaller bag is filled with a few handfuls of hops and both bags are hung in a large pot with 373 g. of syrup. The contents are boiled for 2 hours. (There is no mention of how much water is added but the two bags must have been well covered.)

The bags are then removed, squeezed out, and 35 g. of yeast added to the liquid. The wort is covered and left for a few days to ferment.

The beer was drunk within a few days of brewing as it frequently went sour thereafter. As if encouragement were needed, the imbibers sang:

> "*Tünn, Tünn Tafelbeer,*
> *morgen heff wi Sötbeer*
> *öwermorgen suur Beer.*"

> "*Drink, drink the table beer,*
> *Tomorrow we'll have boiled beer,*
> *The day after, sour beer.*"

Did they boil the beer, rather as one does broth, to stop it going off? According to Baum, they also sang:

> "*Bier, Bier — dat makt Pläsir.*"

Such appalling rhymes are typical of very strong if hastily prepared beers!

m)   THURINGIA BEER. 1804.

This book owes so much to Johann Gottfried Hahn, that it is only fitting that his recipe from Erfurt in East German Thüringen, should bring up the rear. Hahn left no stone unturned so I have shortened his description to about one tenth the original length. Again a mash tub with a tap is required (12).

i)   Take enough soft water and bring it to the boil.

ii)   Allow it to cool until you can just put your hand in it.

iii)   Add the pale malt to produce a thick porridge and stir vigorously for 15 minutes and then stand for a further 15.

iv)   During this time, bring another pot of water of similar volume to the boil.

vi)   Pour the boiling water onto the mash and stir vigorously.

vii)   Leave the mash to stand until the liquid above the malt has become clear. This will take about 1 hour.

viii) Run the liquid off the bottom. Stop as soon as cloudy wort comes through.

ix) Prepare the clear wort for boiling. Mash the draff again (vi-viii).

x) Sparge the draff as normal.

xi) Boil both worts. Hahn did them separately. The hops were boiled in some of the thin sparge water at a rate of 1 pound of hops in 4 ltr. of wort. Alternatively, make a hop extract by soaking the hops in cold water for several hours and then boiling them in the same water for about 30 minutes. Add this to the cooled wort.

xii) Dilute and ferment the wort out using a bottom fermenting yeast at about 8°C.

xiii) Keg the beer and store until clear.

10. Unhopped Beers.

The first references to hops being used in beer date from Charlemagne's reign and they were not known in England until nearly 800 years later. Any serious study of historical beers must ask the question "what was beer like before hops?" Because unhopped beers survived in many places into the late Middle Ages, there is no shortage of material about what spices were used, how, and what effect they had on the drinking public. Hops finally achieved their monopoly in beer brewing because of their disinfecting qualities, but other herbs were used not only in order to produce a variety of tastes. Beer offered a means of taking the herbs for medicinal purposes but was also the conveying medium in man's never ending quest for narcotic and hallucinatory drugs. One finds in historical literature many warnings about the health risks involved in using such herbs but little evidence that a hard core were seriously dissuaded from their use. Times actually change little. It was common to try and increase the effect of the alcohol, or produce drinks which went further than mere intoxication, by adding substances which we regard as severe poisons.

Astute and dishonest publicans also added a variety of substances which increased the thirst of their patrons and equally reprehensible was the practice of adding certain herbs whose taste covered that of spoilt beer. If we imagine the worst possible case of a publican who used narcotic drugs to inebriate, as well as those which increased the thirst in a camouflaged gone off brew, then it was a wonder the drinkers ever got up again. No doubt some didn't!

How and which herbs were used changed during the centuries, as did opinions as to the effects of the different herbs. The frequent references to "bush" in pub names is supposed to refer to the use of ground ivy in the "grout" or herb mixture. The herb mixtures of the Reformation can be gleaned from the 15th century hand written Low German text, a translation of which is provided at the end of this chapter. The fact that the Dutch were at the forefront of plant cultivation at that time and for many years after gives this text an especial historical importance.

In 1691 Tryon discussed the use of hop substitutes and the dangers of some of them. Hahn in 1804 provided an informative scale of usefulness of various herbs. He differentiated between "hop surrogates" i.e. those which produce the same taste and effects as hops, and those which should only be taken on medical advice. He also provided a list of substances which improve the quality of beer (or mask the lack of it) and these he divides into harmful and non-harmful to the health. Many medicinal herbs occur in the following list and it is essential that one consults a modern book on this subject before trying any out, (e.g. Medicinal Plants and their Uses, by Prof. Flück). The seeds of many herbs in the following alphabetical list can be obtained from any good seed merchant. The spices are usually available from health food shops.

Herbs which were frequently used in beer.

ALECOST *Chrysanthemum balsamita.*

This small yellow flowered member of the aster family was a widely used beer spice. It also found favour in the kitchen, for its leaves, when crushed emit a powerful aroma of menthol, melissa and sage. Apart from the obvious medicinal uses it went into the soup and meat pots.

ALEHOOF *Glechoma hederacea.*

The common name is Ground Ivy, and in some parts it is known as the rockery plant Creeping Jenny. It is bitter and aromatic and was the most common hop forerunner. Gerard recorded in 1597 its use in ale in Wales and Cheshire. It "strengthens and cleanses", if that's what you need.

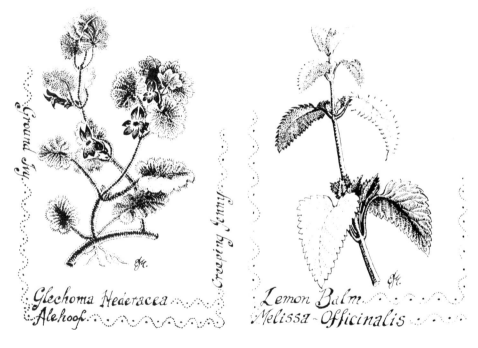

ALOE *Aloes*

Not exactly a native of the UK but Hahn recommends its bitter juice as a hop surrogate. Unless you holiday in Greece or on the Steppes you won't find it outside your local botanical garden. The best bet is to buy the tincture, which should be easily obtained through a pharmacist.

BALM *Melissa officinalis.*

Far too little is known in the UK of this beautiful herb. It isn't a native of Britain but is widely used across Europe in herb liqueurs, salads, and as a tea surrogate. Bees love it and it is supposed to be good against period pains, as a stomach strengthener and to remove melancholy, cheer the heart, drive away heaviness of mind, sharpen the wit and improve the memory. In short, a Mediaeval anti-depressant.

BETONY *Stachys officinalis.*

"'Tis hot, dry acrid and bitter." wrote Pechey but Hahn doesn't mention its use as a hop surrogate. Only Tryon thought highly of this herb, but in the 17th century, Betony was thought to be a cure-all. Grigson describes it as a fraud, with no medicinal value worth mentioning. This may explain its fall from favour.

BOG MYRTLE *Myrica gale.*

This was a well known plant right across North Europe but its habitats have become few due to the draining of marsh and fenlands. Its use in beer is reputed to have caused rapid drunkenness but this apart it was a mainstay of the North German "Grut". It was popular in England too where apart from its use in brewing it was laid in the linen to keep away the fleas.

BUCKBEAN *Menyanthes trifoliata*

This plant too has the bitter taste of the hop and like Bog Myrtle likes a wet environment. Grigson and Hahn record its use in beer as do the Low German sources. As a medicine it was used against jaundice, ague and rheumatism and the German name suggests it may relieve a fever.

CARDUUS *Carduus Benedictus.*

Also known as "Wild Field Saffron", this is reputed to provide a nearly identical bitterness to hops. It grows throughout the year in many fields and according to Hahn is a most valuable hop surrogate. It is not however a native of the British Isles. Its close relation, Milk Thistle, *Silybum marianum* is common enough to be mentioned in Grigson, the bitterness being contained in the stalks.

CENTAURY *Centaurium minus or Gentiana centaurium.*

The root of this medicinal plant is used to provide the bitter taste. Take care though as it may "open the stoppings of the liver, gall and spleen". (Gerard)

COMFREY *Symphytum officinale.*

This beautiful and thankful plant attracts bees like no other to its gentle purple or white flowers. It enjoyed a revival in the sixties, becoming something of a flower-power cure-all. There are many specialist herb books devoted just to this plant but none I have read substantiate Gerards opinion.

"The slimie substance of the root made in a posset of ale, and given to drink against the paine in the backe, gotten by any violent motion, as wrestling or over much use of women, doth in fower or five daies perfectly cure the same, although the involuntarie flowing of the seed in men be gotten thereby."

Betony
Stachys Officinalis

Bog Myrtle
Myrica Gale

Sweet Gale

Blessed Thistle
Cnicus Benedictus

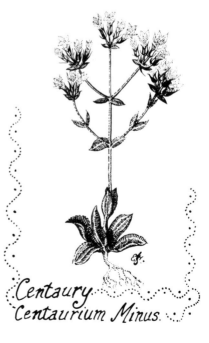

Centaury
Centaurium Minus

DANDELION *Taraxacum officinale*.

The young leaves may be used in salads but agricultural workers in wine producing areas spice their wine with it while in England the steel makers and miners put it in their beer, presumably because of its diuretic properties.

ELECAMPANE *Inula helenium*.

This is another cure-all, the roots of which were commonly infused or boiled with wine and drunk against asthma, coughs, concoction and the plague. It forces urine, cures hip gout and the worms as well as improving the sight. Equestrian brewers will be pleased to learn that it is also a powerful horse medicine. Its use as a beer spice seems to have been more common on the Continent, appearing in Hahn's list of surrogates and in the Low German recipes.

EYEBRIGHT *Euphrasia officinalis*.

As the name implies, this herb was used against the dimming of the eyes and is mentioned in this context in "Paradise Lost", as the plant which revealed to Adam mankind's miserable future. Did Milton use Eyebright to try and cure his own blindness? If so, then apparently without success. "Can there be misery loftier than mine?" he asked.

Pechey was more modest in his claims for this pleasant little weed. Eyebright was served in table-beer "when the eye is much bruis'd", and Tryon simply liked the flavour.

HOREHOUND *Marrubium vulgare*.

The common German name "Berghopfen" (mountain hops) gives it all away. It is still used against coughs, etc. and tastes a little too medicinal for inclusion in my beer.

HYSSOP *Hyssopus officinalis*.

This little known aromatic bush is mentioned in the Bible as the branch used to reach Jesus the vinegar soaked sponge. Benedictine monks brought it to Europe and use its aromatic bitterness in herb liqueurs.

LAVENDER *Lavandula vera*.

Schall uniquely describes lavender as the "je ne sais quoi, of hare and bacon basted in red wine". I doubt one would fail to recognise it in beer so beware! A little will do.

MARJORAM *Origanum vulgare*.

Hahn complained that it lacks the necessary bitterness to be put in beer and perhaps that is why it is used in conjunction with buckbean and woodruff in the Low German recipes. The Italians do wonderful things with its close relation oregano so if you are into herb beers then it must be worth a try.

MUGWORT *Artemisia vulgaris*.

"A medical and magical herb" Grigson calls it. Its availability along the roadsides of Europe make it an obvious choice as a spice. It does not have the bitterness we expect from a beer herb.

Elecampane
Inula Helenium.

Eyebright.
Euphrasia Officinalis.

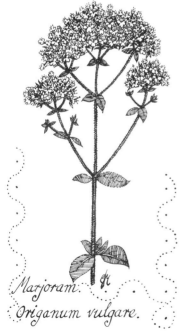

Marjoram.
Origanum vulgare.

Horehound.
Marrubium vulgare.

NETTLE *Urtica dioica*

Another cure-all! Gout to baldness it is reputed to stave off. Nowadays it is taken by the hardy as a tea, salad or flagellation. It is a close relative of the hop and is bitter, especially when mature!

PENNYROYAL *Mentha pulegium.*

This was known across Europe as a herb to induce labour and cure constipation. It was widely used in Britain in pies, puddings and haggis. Only Tryon put it in beer, and why not? Perhaps he didn't suffer from fleas, for driving them out was its other major use.

SAGE *Salvia officinalis.*

This most revered of herbs in Britain and Mediterranean lands is met with wailing and nashing of teeth in Germany. There it's infused as a tea and served with honey to cure coughs, and tastes, I'm reliably informed, disgusting. Sage enjoys a good pedigree though. Charlemagne had it put on his list of Regal Kitchen Herbs and it appears in the Low German recipes as well as in Tryon as a beer spice.

SLOES/BLACKTHORN *Prunus spinosa.*

The leaves make tea, the plums and juice of the flowers go into medicine and of course the plums go into gin.

TANSY *Tanacetum vulgare.*

This beautiful plant has been demoted to weed status. A travesty! Culpepper wrote, "Let those Women who desire Children love this Herb. Tis their best Companion, their Husband excepted". Boiled in beer it "stayed miscarriages".

Tansey.
Tanacetum vulgare

Woodruff.
Asperula odorata.

Hahn mentions Tansy, along with its cousin *tanacetum balsamita*, as hop surrogates. Although they have the right degree of bitterness, he complains of unpleasant side-tastes.

VALERIAN *Valeriana officinalis.*

Commonly drunk as a tea on the Continent for it is supposed to calm the nerves and prevent hysteria, i.e. a mild sedative. Read about it in Flück before you try it!

WOODRUFF *Asperula odorata.*

Woodruff is picked in May, dried a day and then hung for five minutes in white wine, to make the German drink *Maibowle*. According to Gerrard, this was common in England too, "to make a man merrie". Why did we ever stop? The smell of the drying herb and the taste of the wine are quite exquisite. The Berliners hang a little bundle for a few minutes in their wheat beer and all power to their elbows. Grigson says that tea of the wild flowers is also delicious.

Wood Sage
Teucrium scorodonia.

Wormwood.
Artemesia absinthium.

WOOD SAGE *Teucrium scorodonia.*

Grigson tells us the bitter leaves were used in ales before hops arrived in Britain but he provides no details and wood sage appears not to have excited other writers.

WORMWOOD *Artemesia absinthium or Absinthium vulgare.*

Since antiquity, the indispensable slightly bitter taste of this herb has been valued for its beneficial effect on the stomach and intestine. It was mainly served in wine or beer (Pechey 1694) or as a stomach opener prior to eating. (Tryon). The Low German recipes include Wormwood but Hahn isn't so sure. When used as the only spice, it reduces the storage life of the beer (he says) and for some reason he thought it bad for the health.

YARROW *Achillea millefolium*

Yarrow is mentioned by Grigson as one of the herbs which hops replaced. That said, it seems to have enjoyed no other culinary use and in the garden has been demoted to a herb for starting the compost! Medicinally yarrow is still highly thought of. Some say it has more healing substances than Ginseng. It is good against stomach and bowel problems, aids digestion, heals wounds and inflammations of every sort, helps sclerosis, cleans the air pipes and cures any number of women's problems. Alcohol should be avoided during a yarrow cure! Keep the ale thin.

Yarrow.
Achillea millefolium.

Herbs reputed to have narcotic potency.

All the following herbs are mentioned in various books or articles because their addition to beer increased the intoxicating potency. TAKE CARE! It is far more easy to land in hospital than in Seventh Heaven. Remember that communities that regularly used such herbs had the necessary skill to dose them and a common error nowadays is to expect an immediate effect. When none arrives the temptation is to use more of the drug which can be extremely dangerous.

Most interesting is the fact that brewers were often powerless to prevent some of these herbs going into the brew as their seeds could not be easily separated from the barley. They would then be malted with the barley to the detriment of the beer. The most famous incidence of this occurred in the middle ages. If rye or other grasses were attacked by the spores from the parasitic mould *claviceps purpure*, instead of forming starch, the seed filled with ergotomine, ergotoxine, etc. These alkaloids were in common use to prevent bleeding after childbirth, assist in uterine contractions, against migrane and high blood pressure. The peasants were unable to sort every grain harvested to remove the blighted seed and so bread was baked and beer brewed. "Ergotism" or the effect of an overdose, soon began. Paralysis, lack of feeling in the limbs, burning swellings, shaking and violent cramp were the symptoms. The latter sufferings were called "ignis sacer" (holy fire) or St. Anthony's fire, after the saint who tried to help those afflicted. A part of the "Isenheimer Altar" by Mathias Grünewald depicts St. Anthony's work. Some historians have tried to link harvests where ergotism was prevalent, to popular peasant uprisings and so the results of such narcotic substances finding their way into food and drink, cannot be overstated!

DARNEL *Lolium temulentum.*

Darnel grows as a weed among corn and thus used to be harvested with the barley. When malted and used for brewing it was said to produce a beer of a most intoxicating nature and seems to have been most readily tolerated.

MELILOT *Melilotus altissima.*

Likened to woodruff by Grigson, because it contains the same ingredient coumarin. Why 18th century brewers should have complained so bitterly of the effect the seeds of this fine clover had on the drinking public, I do not know. Its medicinal uses are well defined and the dried flowers were used in poultices and plasters. It was the seeds however which caused the following wrath. "it makes the Drink so heady that it is apt to Fuddle the Unwary by drinking a small quantity" and further, "it causes fevers, colics and other distempers of the body," wrote an anonymous 19th century London publican.

THORN APPLE *Datura stramomium.*

"Narcotic, poisonous weed," says Grigson "the strength to knock you out and according to the circumstances, causes fevers, convulsions and even fury", warns Hahn. It was common in the 18th and 19th centuries to add caraway seeds to the beer and many unscrupulous dealers ground thorn apple seeds and sold them as caraway. Pechey in the 17th century maintained that when taken in beer, the ensuing madness could last up to a day and was given by thieves to those whom they intended to rob. The same author continues, "Wenches give half a dram of it to their lovers, in beer or in wine. Some are so skilled in dosing of it, they can make men mad for as many hours as they please." I have known students try this, one of them a pharmacist's son. He received no sympathy with his tea in the local hospital!

Hahn finishes with a series of plants of such power, narcotic and poisonous potency, that it is no wonder that strict legal controls were introduced. What he did ask was why house-brewing was so suppressed thus leaving the unwary drinker at the mercy of villains prepared to lace the beer with opium or strychnine! Certainly one has to view the drinking habits of our forefathers in a quite different light.

Some spices for beer.

Müller records the use of the following spices to improve the bouquet of a beer.

Juniper berries, which are the most popular spice used to flavour North German Schnaps, coriander seed, elder flowers, which make a very fine tea, lime blossoms and orange peel. One crushes the berries and either cooks them with the wort or much better, hangs a linen bag containing the crushed seeds or dried flowers in the beer shortly before drinking it.

Nutmeg, cloves, Seville oranges, cinnamon, and vanilla are also highly recommended additions to beer but Hahn warns against the habit of adding liquorice, camphor, mustard seeds and salt as these increase the thirst the more one drinks.

Historical recipes with herbs and spices.

The techniques involved in making a spiced beer shouldn't be too different from making a hopped beer, but in the same way as hops have to be dried and cooked in the wort for a certain length of time, so other herbs have to be picked, dried and utilized according to their special properties. Once the herbs have been picked and dried, they should be added to a basic ale wort prepared as described. Take an ale recipe which suits the water in your area.

The following Low German recipes are from an anonymous 15th century brewer and have been translated as faithfully as possible. He never suggests boiling the beer with the herbs. Perhaps firewood was in short supply.

"Those there who want to make Old Beer, which is also called Shavings Beer, let him take and plane shavings from dry fir wood, put them in a pot and boil them well and lay them afterward in a loft and dry them well, but not in the sun. Then bind them in a small bundle and put them in the beer. In any case the shavings make every beer pure and clear. If you want to make herb beer, then take Marjoram, Buckbean, and Woodruff and from these three make a small bundle and put them in the beer.

If you want to make Sage, Hyssop or Lavender Beer so pick these herbs between the days of Our Good Lady's Ascension and Birth (15.8-8.9) and dry these herbs completely in a loft, but not in the sun but in the air. When they are dry, rub them and put them in a bag and hang them half depth in the beer. If you want the beer stronger then hang the bag deeper in the beer. If you want to keep the herbs then take the bag out and hang it in the air to dry completely and hang it in another beer. This way you will make a strong beer which keeps for every occasion.

If you want to make Cherry Beer then let the cherries become fully ripe and black and beat them to pieces in the beer vat and leave them in the vat overnight. Squeeze the cherry meat through a sieve so that the stones are removed and the fruit is made smaller. Then put the cherry fruit into a cloth and

Sage
Salvia officinalis

Hyssop.
Hyssopus officinalis.

Lavender.
Lavandula vera.

pull this through the beer to give the beer colour. Then take the stones and dry them in the air but first rub them thoroughly between the hands. When they are dry break them with a stone and bind the pieces in a bag and hang them halfway in the beer. If you want the beer right strong then take many bags for the stones give the beer the strength and colour it strong. Then the beer stays strong but you must shake it every year.

If you want Sloe Beer so pick the Sloes at Michaelmas (29.9.) when they are not too ripe. Wood Sloes are best. Break the Sloes with a stone and beat them until they are soft. Put them as they are, with their skins into a bag with some salt, into the beer. If you want to do a whole barrel of beer then take three bowls of sloes and put them all in.

If you want Valerian Beer then dry half a pound of good Valerian roots, put them in a bag and put this in the beer. They should remain in the beer for three weeks. Take the bag out in the third week, let it dry and then hang it in again.

If you want Elecampane Beer, then dig the roots between Ascension Day and the Birth of Our Lady, clean them and put them in a bag. According to how strong you want the beer hang more or less of the root in. The roots must be clean and dried, not in the sun, but in a loft or cupboard where there is no draught.

If you want to make Mugwort Beer, then pick wild Mugwort and dry it as described, not in the sun but in a loft where much air goes through. Bind it in a little bundle and hang this in the beer.

The same should be done to make Wormwood Beer. Pick it between the two Feasts of Our Lady, fully dry it away from the sun and leave it in the beer a half, or even a whole year and look often to see that it does grow no mould.

All these beers should be served every evening. The beer should not be cloudy but clear and not too young. If you do this well and you have a good beer then you will always be a good host.

If you want to clear a cloudy beer, then take dry beech wood with the bark still on and dry it in the air in a loft or chamber, but not in the sun. Plane as thin shavings from it as you can and bind them to a bundle and lay this in the beer and it will become clear and pure".

Additional herbs which were preferred to hops.

The following ideas were recorded by Thomas Tryon in his 1691 edition of "A New Art of Brewing Ale and other Liquors". This author suggests two principle ways of spicing beer. One way is to mix the desired herbs with an unhopped young beer 15 minutes before it is to be served, probably hanging the herbs in bundles directly in the beer, or if the leaves are small and difficult to bundle, then with the help of a linen (or cotton) bag. Obviously the herbs cannot develop the disinfecting qualities obtained by boiling the wort over an hour with hops and one must assume that the beer was consumed at one or two sittings. The other method was to leave the herbs for 30 minutes in the still warm,

Sloes, Blackthorn.
Prunus spinosa.

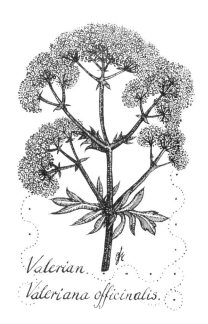

Valerian.
Valeriana officinalis.

Mugwort.
Artemisia vulgaris.

unhopped wort. If many herbs were to be used then they would be dipped in one after another, never several bundles of different herbs at the same time. In many types of cuisine, the order in which the spices are added and the time interval between additions is most important, but there is no mention of such refinements in brewing literature.

Both these methods can be used for pennyroyal, balm, ground ivy, fennel, caraway or coriander seeds. (As the latter three cannot have been known long in England when Tryon wrote his book, I suspect this is where he took his title from.) Tansy, wormwood, eyebright, betony, sage, dandelion as well as good hay, are better laid 30 minutes in the beer.

Tryon also has a novel suggestion for a Lent breakfast drink. Add seventy drops of brandy to a glass of ale the evening before.

Nettle, Dandelion or Comfrey Beer.

The following Leicester recipe was recorded in 1927 but is probably as old as beer itself. It uses all three plants but this is a matter of taste. It is the method which is of interest.

Wort 1 gallon; whole ginger bruised 1 oz.; nettles 2 or 3 handfuls; also a few dandelions, and some comfrey.

- Boil the wort.
- Add the well washed nettles, dandelions and comfrey. Boil for 15 minutes.
- Strain off the liquor.
- Boil it up with the ginger and strain again.
- Cream 1 oz. of compressed yeast, put it on a piece of toast and lay it in the liquor when lukewarm.
- Let it stand till the next morning covered in a warm place.
- Take off the scum and bottle without disturbing the sediment.

It was probably stored some time. There is no mention if dandelion and comfrey leaves or roots were used. It may have been either, depending on the time of year.

Using Buckbean instead of Hops.

Hahn describes in detail the use of Buckbean as a hop surrogate which is cheap and healthy. The method is generally applicable to other herbs.

"One lets the buckbean boil in water for a few minutes and then discards the bitter brew. Then cook the leaves for another hour in fresh water and strain. Add half of this extract to the first wort (see German recipes) and boil for 1

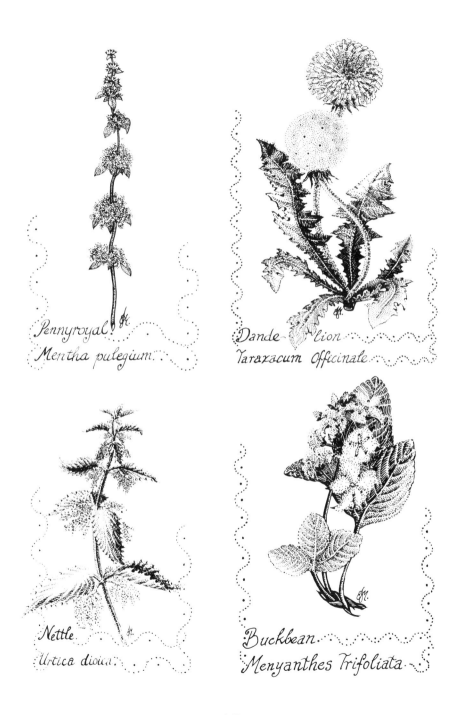

Pennyroyal
Mentha pulegium

Dandelion
Taraxacum Officinale

Nettle
Urtica dioica

Buckbean
Menyanthes Trifoliata

143

hour. Decide if the wort is going to be bitter enough. If not, add from the rest of the Buckbean extract to the other worts. If, against expectation, the beer is not bitter enough, add the extract a spoonful at a time, to the maturing beer when it is in the barrels. To one bucket of beer (about 70 tankards probably of 0.5 ltr.) 10-12 Loth (1 Loth is about 14 g.) Buckbean are used. Before fermentation one cannot drink such a beer, but immediately it has fermented out it loses the harsh bitterness. Such beer never becomes sour and may be kept for years and thus one can brew in reserve, but it must ferment right out.

In England Buckbean has been used for many years instead of hops, in double and other beers, which because of their unique taste are called Porters".

Thus Hahn gives us yet another definition of a porter. I'm not sure he was right. He also records the following usage of some spices.

"Mix some starch and mace into the beer just as the fermentation is beginning. This is very agreeable, improves the strength and taste and gets the fermentation going better".

The amount of mace used is a matter of taste but it shouldn't be too much.

Juniper Berries deserve above all other things to be added to beer. He continues:

"To one bucket add 2-3 Loth of selected, fresh, black Juniper Berries. Crush them and add them to the wort when it has nearly finished boiling. Alternatively, one can add the crushed Juniper in the cellar. Put them in a linen sack and hang them in the maturing beer for a few days and then remove them. Such beer has a pleasant taste, is healthy and promotes the urine.

In a similar way one can improve the taste of beer by adding cloves (called "spicey nails" by Hahn,) nutmeg, cinnamon, vanilla, lemons, seville oranges and such spices. None of these additions are bad for the health, on the contrary, they are beneficial and pleasant".

APPENDIX 1

Increasing permanent hardness

Increasing the permanent hardness involves adding calcium and magnesium sulphates and allows us to use dark malts for brewing the typical darker types of beer. Dortmund water contains 240 mg/ltr. sulphate ion and as can be seen from the table, comes from a typical dark beer area.

ANALYSIS OF SOME FAMOUS BREWING WATERS.

Amount (mg/ltr.)	Munich	Pilsen	Dortmund	Vienna	Lingen
Calcium ion Ca^2	75	70	262	162	–
Magnesium ion Mg^2	18	0.72	23	67	–
Sulphate ion $SO_4{}^{2-}$	7.5	4.3	240	180	50
Hydrogen Carbonate $HCO_3{}^-$	310	27.7	366	690	122
Chloride ion Cl^-	2	5	107	39	1
Temporary hardness (carbonate)	high	low	high	v. high	moderate
Permanent hardness (sulphate)	v. low	v. low	high	moderate	low
Total hardness	high	v. low	high	v. high	low

Every gram of calcium sulphate, will contain 230 mg. calcium ions, 560 mg. sulphate ions and water. Thus we require slightly less than 0.5 g/ltr. calcium sulphate to achieve Dortmund levels of sulphate ion concentration. Now kitchen scales may be accurate to the nearest ounce (approx. 30 g.) but it would be unusual, so there is no point trying to weigh the salt. By knowing the solubility of various salts, a Dortmund water can be imitated. The following calculations assume the water contains no naturally occurring sulphate ions. This will rarely be the case and so allowance must be made. An accurate water analysis from the water board is essential before starting.

1) Take 1 ltr. of cold water and stir in calcium sulphate until no more dissolves. It won't take much calcium sulphate. The tip of a teaspoon is an appropriate start.

2) This produces a saturated solution containing about 2 g/ltr. You want about 30 ltr. of water to make your beer, each litre containing 0.5 g. of the salt so

the water in the jug contains enough calcium sulphate to make 4 ltr. of brewing water.

3) Decant your salt water into a large container (leaving the undissolved salt in the measuring jug) and add another 3 ltr. of tap water to the container. You now have 4 ltr. of water of Dortmund concentration.

4) Repeat the exercise another 7 times and you have 28 ltr. of Dortmund water.

One more example!

Magnesium sulphate has the solubility 355 g/ltr. 1 g. of magnesium sulphate (Epsom Salts, the hepta hydrate) contains 100 mg. magnesium ions, 390 mg. sulphate ions and water. To achieve Vienna water we need 180 mg/ltr. sulphate ion or 180 divided by 390 grams of magnesium sulphate, i.e. about 0.5 g.

1) Stir 40 g. or just over 1 ounce of magnesium sulphate into 100 cm³ water. When no more dissolves, the solution is saturated and contains 36 g. of salt.

2) Pour off the solution leaving the undissolved salt behind in the measuring beaker.

3) Dilute the magnesium sulphate solution to 1 ltr. Your concentration is now 3.6 g/ltr.

4) Pour this into your large vat and add another 6 ltr. of water. Your concentration is 0.5 g/ltr. and you have 7 ltr. of brewing water.

5) Repeat four more times and you have enough Vienna water to brew with.

MAKING TEMPORARY HARD WATER.

Temporary hard water contains dissolved calcium hydrogen carbonate which cannot be purchased because it doesn't exist as a solid, but only in solution. You can buy it as mineral water and the amount of dissolved calcium hydrogen carbonate is often given on the label so you can calculate the necessary dilution. It probably isn't worth it. Temporary as well as permanent hardness allow the brewing of dark beers and I advise only trying to adjust the latter. Don't try to compensate for lack of temporary hardness by adding permanent hardness salts.

REMOVING TEMPORARY HARDNESS.

Boil the water for ten minutes and the calcium hydrogen carbonate will be precipitated as insoluble calcium carbonate. Doing this reduces the alkalinity of the water and makes it unsuitable for dark beers, but good for strongly hopped and pale beers. You must reduce the amount of hops used if the water contains "carbonate" hardness. Some writers claim that more than 150 mg/ltr. calcium hydrogen carbonate concentration renders the water unsuitable for brewing as the hops take on a rough bitterness which is quite unpleasant. Luers writes about Munich water which contains 310 mg/ltr. hydrogen carbonate ion: "It affords a dark, full bodied beer which is very easy on the palate" (i.e. use lots of dark malt and not much hops). Pilsen water is very soft and he says of it: "This allows a pale beer of strongly accentuated noble hop-bitterness". i.e. use pale malt and shovel the hops in!

Having set up these guidelines, study of the recipes will reveal numerous examples where the rules of thumb were ignored.

REMOVING PERMANENT HARDNESS.

This cannot be done in a domestic kitchen as an ion exchange column would be needed. If you want a really soft water and live in an unpolluted area, then you can't do better than rain water. Do test the pH-value though and be sure that it is not too acid from industrial pollution. A cheap source of distilled water is also useful but like rain water will need a few salts added to bring it up to brewing standards.

ADJUSTING THE CHLORIDE ION CONCENTRATION.

The chloride ion concentration of brewing water varies between virtually nothing and about 0.1 g/ltr. The available chloride salts are potassium and sodium chlorides, the latter being table salt. Potassium chloride has a solubility of about 300 g/ltr. and 1 g. contains 500 mg. potassium ions and 500 mg. chloride ions. Sodium chloride has a solubility of about 350 g/ltr. and 1 g. of the salt contains 400 mg. sodium ions and 600 mg. chloride ions. Use of the water analysis table and the method described for adjusting the permanent hardness, can be easily applied.

REMEMBER!

1) Always use cold water to regulate ion concentrations.

2) Salts do not dissolve up immediately so stir in the salt and wait several hours before decanting off the saturated salt solution. Don't warm the water to make the salts dissolve up more quickly.

3) Only adjust the salt ion concentrations if you can do the sums involved.

4) Use only good quality pure salts to add to your brewing water, purchased through a chemist. Table salt is fine for chloride ion adjustments.

5) Don't try to regulate your water without first having studied a water analysis sheet from the local water board and remember to allow for the salts already present when calculating how much of a salt to add.

6) Don't lose sight of the fact that Mesopotamian brewers nearly 6000 years ago, mashed with bread and spiced with honey and dates. They didn't care a fig for water analysis sheets. Hahn in 1804 reported he was happy if he didn't have bits of dead plant floating in his beer water.

APPENDIX 2.

Things to do with a hop shoot.

HOPS IN EGG PASTRY.

A pastry is made from:

      125 g. flour
      salt
      0.25 ltr. milk
      1-2 eggs

You also need:

      cooked fresh young hop shoots
      bacon fat
      melted butter

The pastry ingredients are mixed to a smooth dough and fried with a little bacon fat to form very thin cakes. The cooked hop shoots are wrapped in the cakes and served covered in melted butter.

HOP SHOOTS FREIBURG STYLE.

One covers the cooked hop shoots with grated cheese and browned butter.

HOP SHOOTS HUNTER'S STYLE.

One souses the shoots and serves them cold with bacon and mushrooms.

They are also served with any smoked meat, cold pork, hard boiled eggs, omelette, scrambled eggs and any type of sausage.

Don't be afraid to add some of the draff from the mash to the pastry, or to a bread dough. It makes excellent roughage and tastes distinctively toothsome.

APPENDIX 3.

Changes in the barley mass during malting.

During the first phase of malting, the steep, the barley takes up nearly its own weight in water and in the ensuing days of germination and drying, it loses still more. One of the beauties of malting is that the barley behaves in an entirely predictable way and the actual passing through of the various stages can be followed by observation of the mass changes due to the gain, then loss of water. Here is an example from my note book.

16.2.79

$$\text{Mass of barley} = 2.5 \text{ kg.}$$

Assuming 12% water.
    2.5 kg. equivalent to 100%
    y kg. equivalent to 12%

$$2.5/y = 100/12 \quad \text{thus } y = 2.5 \times 12/100$$
$$y = 0.3 \text{ kg.}$$

Thus the dry weight of the barley is 2.5 kg. − 0.3 kg. = 2.2 kg.

19.2.79 (70 hours later).

$$\text{Mass of steeped barley} = 3.9\,\text{kg.}$$
$$\text{Mass of water taken up} = 3.9\,\text{kg.} - 2.2\,\text{kg.} = 1.7\,\text{kg.}$$
$$\text{\% water in steeped barley} = 1.7/3.9 \times 100$$
$$= 43.5\%$$

This figure is well within the limits of accuracy of my kitchen scales.

25.2.79

Germination complete with 95% of a sample of 180 grains showing acrospires approximately ⅔ of the corn length.

$$\text{Mass of green malt} = 3.715\,\text{kg.}$$
$$\text{Mass of water in green malt} = 3.175\,\text{kg.} - 2.2\,\text{kg.} = 0.975\,\text{kg.}$$
$$\text{\% water in green malt} = 0.975/3.715 \times 100$$
$$= 30.7\%$$

28.2.79

Mass of malt after drying and roasting = 1.915 kg.

As I started with a dry weight of 2.2 kg., I assume that the mass loss due to respiration and reduction in water content must be

$$2.5\,\text{kg.} - 1.915\,\text{kg.} = 0.585\,\text{kg.}$$
$$\text{\% loss in mass during malting} = 0.585/2.5 \times 100$$
$$= 23\%$$

I based my home malter on the description of a pneumatic malter by Dr. Paul Dreverhoff. I was naturally delighted to find that in his sample the mass loss was 24%. I quote his figures:

$$\text{Mass of air dried barley} = 100\,\text{kg.}$$
$$\text{Mass of steeped barley} = 148\,\text{kg.}$$
$$\text{Mass of green malt} = 140\,\text{kg.}$$
$$\text{Mass of freshly dried malt} = 76\,\text{kg.}$$
$$\text{Mass of stored malt} = 78\,\text{kg.}$$

The loss may vary between 19-27% but on average is between 20-25%.

If we achieve losses within these limits then we are controlling the malting process as well as the professional malster.

Dreverhoff also summarises the reasons for these losses:

Difference in water content of barley and malt	= 10-12%
Losses through leaching in the steep	= 0.6-1.5%
Losses through cleaning off roots, etc.	= 3.5-6%
Losses through respiration	= 5-8%

Total losses are 19.1-27.5%

Density, Relative Density and Hydrometers.

The density of a substance is given by the quotient:

mass of substance/volume of substance

Thus the units of density are g/cm³ or kg/m³ etc.

Relative density, which has in the past also gone under the names "specific weight", "specific density" and "gravity" is more usual in brewing circles because it is dimensionless. It is the density of any substance divided by the density of water.

The relative density of a sugar solution with an actual density of 1.100 g/cm³ is:

$$1.100 \text{ g/cm}^3/1.000 \text{ g/cm}^3$$

The units cancel, leaving a relative density   = 1.100

As all relative densities which occur in brewing are in the range 0.900-1.200, some brewers further simplify life by leaving the unit and decimal point out, and expressing relative densities in whole number degrees. Thus a relative density of 1.045 becomes 45 degrees. On the side of some beer cans one reads, "Initial Gravity = 35". This means that the relative density of the wort, prior to fermentation commencing, was 1.035. In the following calculations all densities are relative, with no units and a decimal point.

There is an approximate relationship between density and percentage concentration of sugar in the wort. Although we don't know how much of the dissolved material is fermentable sugar and how much is non-fermentable protein or starch, etc. this does allows us to relate the density of the wort to the amount of alcohol which may be expected from it after fermentation. Many hydrometers have three scales on their sides:- the density; the weight of sugar which would produce this density and the percentage alcohol which may be expected from that much sugar.

DILUTING THE WORT PRIOR TO FERMENTATION.

Supposing mash and sparge produces 15 ltr. wort with a potential alcohol content of 6.5% and the required alcohol content is 4.5%.

Adding water then should give y ltr. of wort with a potential alcohol content of 4.5%.

$$y \quad = \quad 6.5/4.5 \times 15 \text{ ltr.}$$
$$y \quad = \quad 21.61 \text{ ltr.}$$

The final volume of the wort, before fermentation, should be around 21 ltr.

ADDING SUGAR.

Any dilution should take place after the wort has been cooked with the hops, cooled, and strained. Any additional sugar however should be added prior to boiling the wort, although this is by no means essential. 1 kg. of household sugar dissolved in 10 ltr. of wort, will raise the relative density of the wort by 35 degrees. Thus 15 ltr. of wort, with a relative density of 1.045, will go up by:

$$10/15 \times 35 \quad = \quad 23.3 \text{ degrees.}$$

This is equivalent to a relative density rise to 1.023 which when added to the original wort relative density, yields a final value of:

$$1.045 + 0.023 \quad = \quad 1.068$$

The potential alcohol content would go up to around 10%. To get back to a starting gravity suitable for a Pils, one must dilute to a new volume y.

$$y \quad = \quad 10/4.5 \times 15 \text{ ltr.} \quad = \quad 26 \text{ ltr.}$$

Thus 11 ltr. of water must be added.

APPENDIX 5.

Effectiveness of mashing.

The home brewer will always be interested in how effective his mash has been, as this is the main measure of his skill. Theoretically 1 kg. of good light malt can supply 30 degrees of extract to 10 ltr. of mash water. If for example, 15 ltr. of wort of relative density 1.045, were obtained from 2.5 kg. malt, then:

in 10 ltr. water the 2.5 kg. could have supplied $2.5 \times 30 \quad = \quad 75$ degrees.

in 15 ltr. water this becomes $10/15 \times 75 \quad = \quad 50$ degrees.

Our actual relative density was 1.045 or 45 degrees of extract. This is a mash effectivity of: $\quad 45/50 \times 100 \quad = \quad 90\%$

Any home brewer who has mashed with this effectivity from his own malt, may be truly proud. He will have controlled variables such as temperature and pH to a nicety for it is not unusual to achieve effectivities of between 60-70%, especially when making beers which don't suit the water they are being brewed from. The following examples which come from an economic study of brewing in Hall in North Tyrol in the year 1830 are illuminating.

1221 buckets of beer were made from 1182 star of malt and 610 pounds of hops. Converted to modern units, this is equivalent to 300 g. malt for each litre of beer.

The hydrometer hadn't reached Tyrol by then so we don't know too much about the strength of the beer, but the "Magistrat" from Hall praised the skill of the Braumeister and described the brew as a "Doppelbier". It probably then had an alcohol concentration of around 10% and if we assume this to be the case then the mash effectivity was in the order of 77%, and that without thermo-meter, hydrometer or pH-paper. A further study from the same paper reveals that in 1747, 432 g. malt/litre beer were needed. This puts that brewer's mash efficiency at around 54%.

The quantities of hops used is also interesting. About 300 kg. were cooked up in the 1830 brew, which means that about 25 g/ltr. beer was common. These days we think more in terms of 5 g/ltr. beer.

Making a hop and malt drier.

Construct or find a firm wooden box or chest about the size of a domestic baking oven. The front end or top, must be removable to facilitate access to a series of wire drying trays which are placed into the box in the same way as the baking trays are suspended in a baking oven. The wire trays should be about 2 cm. deep and stacked no closer than 15-20 cm. over each other. They should also be slightly shorter than the box to allow good air circulation through the box.

Oblong holes are needed at the bottom front and top rear of the oven to allow a fan heater to blow air through the box. Care must be taken that the air circulation is not so hindered that the elements in the heater over-heat.

A "burst fire proportional controller" kit can be purchased from TK Electronics, 13 Boston Road, London, W7 3SJ. This very reasonably priced piece of electronics will regulate the electric current through the heating elements and thus produce a fine control of the cabinet temperature. DON'T wire the temperature controller to the fan circuit, only to the heating elements! The fan must be free to run on full power whenever the heater is in use. For hop drying and air dried malts, the heater facility will often not be needed and the fan alone will suffice.

Two holes to allow entry of a thermometer are needed to measure the input and exhaust air temperatures. When these are the same, the hops or malt are dry.

Bibliography.

Amsinck, G. S. Practical Brewing. A series of fifty brewings in extenso. London 1868.

"A New Treatise on Liquor", The London Country Brewer, London 1759.

Baum, A. Essen und Trinken im Holsteiner Land.

Bickerdycke, J. The Curiosities of Ale and Beer. 1886

Bock, H. Kreüterbuch. 1577

Bogen, H. J. Knauers Buch der Biotechnik. Droemer Knauer. 1976

Braunfels, W. Abendländische Klosterbaukunst. Verlag Du Mont. Köln. 1969.

Burgess, A. H. Hops: botany, cultivation and utilisation. Leonard Hill. 1964

Childs, S. Everyman his own Brewer. London, 1798.

Crecelius, W. Rezepte für bereitung von kräuterbiere. Jahrbuch für niederdeutsche Sprachforschung, 4 (1878)

Crell, L. Vorschläge zu neuen Vortheilen beim Bierbrauen. Translated from an English edition by Richardson. J. Berlin, 1788

Dodoens, R. Crüyde Boek. 1644

Dreverhoff, P. Brauereiwesen I. Mälzerei. Leipzig, 1906.

"Every Family's Cookery Book". Undated and without Authoress. William Nicholson & Son, Wakefield.

Flück, H. Medicinal Plants and their uses. Foulsham, Bucks, 1976

Ford. Treatise on malting and brewing. London, 1862

Fuchs, L. Neu Kreüterbuch. 1543

Gerard, J. The Herbal or Generall Historie of Plantes. 1597

Grigson G. The Englishman's Flora. Granada Publishing Ltd. St. Albans, 1975.

Hahn. J. G. Die Hausbrauerei. Erfurt, 1804.

Hoffmann, M. 5000 Jahre Bier. Alfred Metzner Verlag, Frankfurt am Main, 1956.

Juch, J. Die Hauptbedingnisse um ein gutes Bier zu brauen. Etlinger'scher Verlagsbuchhandlung, Würzburg, 1842.

Knaust, H. Von Eigenschaften der Biere. 1575.

Laux, H. & H. Kochbuch für Pilzfreunde. Franckh. Stuttgart, 1980

Loewenfeld, C. Herb Gardening. Faber. London, 1974

Lüers, H. Brauereiwesen I. Mälzerei. W. de Gruyter & Co. Berlin, 1923.

Lüers, H. Die Wissenschaftlichen Grundlagen von Mälzerei und Brauerei. Verlag Hans Karl, Nürnberg, 1950.

Mathias, P. The Brewing Industry in England 1700-1830. Cambridge, 1959.

Monckton, H. A. A History of English Ales and Beers. The Bodley Head Ltd. 1966.

Müller, A. E. Lehrbuch der Ober- und Untergährung des Bieres. Viehweg & Sohn, Braunschweig, 1845.

Münzing-Ruef, I. So heilt die Natur. Heyne, München, 1983

Neunlinger, B. Tiroler Wirtschaftsstudien 2. Folge, Die Brauereien von Hall in Tirol im 16.-19. Jahrhundert. Universitätsverlag Wagner, Innsbruck, 1956.

Parkes. The Domestic Brewer. London, 1821.

Pechey, J. The Compleat Herbal of Physical Plants. 1694.

Peers, C. Rievaulx Abbey. HMSO, London.

Richarz, I. Herrschaftliche Haushalte in vorindustrieller Zeit im Weserraum. Berlin, 1971.

Richmond, I. A. Roman Britain. Penguin, 1963.

Schall, S. Köstliches Gewürz. Verlag Mensch und Arbeit, München, 1969.

Schuhholz, A. Köstliche Spezialitäten aus der Schwäbischen Küche. Stuttgart.

Schoellhorn, F. Bibliographie des Brauwesens. Verlagsanstalt Benziger, Einsiedeln (Switzerland), 1926

Shepard, E. H. Drawn from Memory. Penguin, 1976.

Stopes, S. Malt and Malting, F.W. Lyon, London, 1885.

Tryon, T. A New Art of Brewing Ale and other Malt Liquors. 1691.

Watkins, G. The Complete English Brewer. 1770.

White, F. Good things in England. Futura Publications Ltd. London 1974.

INDEX

154

155